SECRETS OF A SIX-FIGURE STYLIST

Secrets of a Six-Figure Stylist
The Beauty Business Blueprint: Strategies for Success

Lacey Broocke & Kylie Phillippi

©2025 All Rights Reserved. No portion of this book may be reproduced, stored in a retrieval system, or transmitted in any form or by any means-electronic, mechanical, photocopy, recording, scanning, or other- except for brief quotations in critical reviews or articles without the prior permission of the author.

Published by Game Changer Publishing

Paperback ISBN: 978-1-964811-53-6
Hardcover ISBN: 978-1-964811-54-3
Digital: ISBN: 978-1-964811-55-0

www.GameChangerPublishing.com

Read This First

Just to say thanks for buying and reading our book, we are giving you "Bonus Resources" to enhance your experience.

You can scan the QR code now or "access as you go" at the end of chapters.

Thank you! Enjoy!

SECRETS OF A SIX-FIGURE STYLIST

The Beauty Business Blueprint:

Strategies for Success

Lacey Broocke & Kylie Phillippi

www.GameChangerPublishing.com

Table of Contents

Introduction 1

Chapter 1 – Mindset and Gratitude 3

Chapter 2 – Become a Magnetic Money Machine 15

Chapter 3 – Essential Elements of Building Your Beauty Brand 29

Chapter 4 – Create an Experience They'll Never Forget 45

Chapter 5 – Work Smarter, Not Harder 63

Chapter 6 – So You Want to Work for Yourself? 83

Chapter 7 – Investing in Yourself 93

Chapter 8 – Smart Financial Management and Exit Strategies 115

Chapter 9 – Take Meaningful Action 137

Final Thoughts… 141

INTRODUCTION

Hi! We're Kylie and Lacey: two wives, mothers, and successful beauty industry leaders who have been living in this salon world for the last twenty-three years. As a couple of "fempreneurs," we think big and aren't afraid to chase after every dream. We have built and owned successful salon companies from scratch, and we learned just as much from our mistakes as we did from our successes. Lacey has spent half of her career educating thousands of salon professionals across the country and has witnessed some recurring gaps in the industry that are still just waiting to be filled. Kylie has also been inspired to help stylists be more successful, either by working with her and her company or by eventually opening up their own businesses.

We think of this industry as our baby; we care for it, we love it, and we live it. More importantly, we want better for our successors than what we had. That's why we decided to write this book. This industry has been keeping the world beautiful for so long and has contributed to so much success. Imagine if Taylor Swift showed up to the Grammys after styling her own hair and makeup. And who remembers what Carrie Underwood looked like on *American Idol* before the glam squad got ahold of her? Need we say more?

In this book, we'll share our stories of grit, grace, and what it takes to be a Six-Figure Stylist. Our hope is to inspire you to be the greatest you can be. Our hope is that you thrive after identifying systems and steps to help you get to where you want to go without burning out. Our hope is to set you up so that no matter what happens, you have a plan for success. Our hope is that you can retire worry-free one day. Our hope is that you know that you have us to lean on as you embark on this journey.

CHAPTER 1

MINDSET AND GRATITUDE

The journey to a successful career and financial abundance all starts with your mindset. Nothing happens by accident. It all starts with intention. You have to be really clear and concise when it comes to what you want. You have to feel it, then visualize and affirm it at least twice a day.

A couple of years ago, Lacey earned an incentive trip from her collagen affiliate company in the form of a trip to Puerto Vallarta. She worked so hard to earn this trip! She lost sleep and became obsessed with her work. Not because she wanted to go that badly; it was because she knew that most of the top earners in the company would be there, and a lot of them were earning more than six figures each month from home without missing a second of their children's lives or any other important events. She knew that they would be willing to share how they'd reached this level of success and that she wanted to make massive changes in her own life in order to do the same. Everyone gave her the same advice: start your day with gratitude!

She didn't know exactly what that meant, but she did know that she needed to change her circle of friends. She'd always heard that the five people you hang out with most make the greatest impact in your life, so she decided to seek out those who lived the life she desired for herself. Upon her arrival, she met an engaged couple. They were going to get married while they were there, so naturally, she congratulated them. Not two hours later, a friend called her to ask if she would do the bride's hair for the wedding. Talk about a divine appointment! Lacey became great friends with the bride as they bonded over wedding hairstyles and shared stories. The bride gifted her a "pay it forward call" with her life coach: someone who had coached over half of the millionaires in that particular company (as well as a few celebrities).

Although she didn't know it at the time, Lacey was really only vibing at about half capacity most days back then, and the life coach, Mr. Bill, helped her to discover that the things she was focusing on were only adding more of what she didn't want to her life. If she wanted to attract more joy and abundance, she was going to have to focus on those things and make a conscious effort to control her thoughts.

> *"Change your thoughts, change your life."*
> – Wayne Dyer

To do this, she had to discover what was really most important to her, or her nine highest values. She had never given that much thought other than to prioritize her relationship with God and her family but acknowledged that her daily to-do lists often didn't get done. She filled her days with tasks, and they weren't even based on what was most important to her. She was unfulfilled, depressed, and stressed. Lacey traveled across the country every weekend while her husband traveled during the week. And while she loved the trips, education, and her career, she loved her family more. She didn't realize that all of that back-and-forth was making her sick until she stopped. She also began planning her days the night before according to her nine highest values. Scheduling in time for gratitude came first, then making sure she had time for everything that was most important to her.

What a difference that made! Within a few months, she began to notice major shifts in her life and had a divine moment in her car when she heard an evangelist on the radio quote the Bible verse that includes, *"I can do **all** things through Christ who gives me strength"* (Philippians 4:13). Although she had heard it a thousand times before, this time was different. He also said, "If I know the Holy Spirit lives in me, then there is nothing I can't do." This made her wonder why she should question herself if she didn't question God. At that moment, she released every limiting belief she had ever entertained about herself and decided that there were no limits to what was possible, only what she previously thought was possible or impossible.

She attracted more joy and opportunities to make drastic changes to her earnings. Her marriage improved, too! In less than six months, she realized that she needed to take a break from traveling and education to focus on the more lucrative opportunities she had closer to home, which she felt could truly make a positive impact on the salons and beauty industry. She knew so many salon owners and beauty professionals who struggled after COVID-19, and most of them didn't even know about the Employment Retention Credit (ERC). The opportunity to make more money by helping salons rake in more placed her in another circle, one that taught her a lot about e-commerce and high-ticket affiliate marketing. Some of the people she met earned millions per month (yes, you read that right), which she'd thought was impossible for the everyday person. And yet, between October and February, she made more money than she had in almost three years combined!

Sometimes, we have to get rid of things to make room for new opportunities. Lacey took charge of her life and turned it into one from which she wouldn't want a vacation. She sold or gave away most of her belongings and moved to the beach, something she'd always dreamt of doing. She had the most beautiful gulf view, and for the first time in her life, she was totally content. She wanted for nothing, even though she didn't physically have much anymore, and she was so very grateful. Then again, it's hard not to be grateful when you can look out your window and see the ocean while you work. But she learned to be grateful for the hard or negative things, too and realized that all of our hardships happen for us, not necessarily to us. Strengthening her relationship with God healed the wounds she'd been living with for years:

childhood trauma, abuse, rape, loss. Now, she is grateful for every event that led her to this present because they shaped who she is.

One can choose to be grateful for all things or miserable. That's the beauty of it; we get to choose the life we want. Life coach Mr. Bill said, "Anger and sadness cannot exist where there is gratitude."

> *"All we have is now. Now is the only moment that can change the course of your life."*
> – Wayne Dyer

The power of positive thinking can have a massive impact on one's business and personal life. Something to note before we continue is your vibration. We've all heard of the law of attraction, but it is actually secondary to the law of vibration. In other words, get your vibe in check. Where your focus goes, your energy flows. So, if we're thinking positively, we're going to see a positive outcome. If we're thinking negatively, we'll get a negative outcome. It's all about what we're thinking, and that brings us to positive, mindful practices that can help you naturally lean more toward a positive mindset. Are you ready to learn about our top visualization and manifestation techniques?

Rule #1: Be specific and concise regarding what you want, not what you don't want. Say out loud whatever it is that you want and give gratitude for it as if you already have it. So, if you want to earn six figures in a month, start expressing gratitude and imagine what it feels like to earn that kind of money.

Rule #2: Visualize what you want and focus on not only what it will look like but how it will make you feel. Hang on to that feeling for at least seventeen seconds. (17 seconds comes from *The Law of Attraction: The*

Basics of the Teachings of Abraham by Esther and Jerry Hicks. 17 seconds represents the time needed to emotionalize the thought.)

Rule #3. Have faith and believe that the universe will start to pull what you desire into your life.

Practicing gratitude plays a significant role in achieving both professional and personal success. Starting and ending—or, as we like to say, bookending—our days with gratitude have changed everything for us.

> *"I walk by faith and not by sight."*
> – (2 Corinthians 5:7)

We believe in creating and repeating positive affirmations based on our nine highest values, but a lot of people don't even realize what their nine highest values are. So, take a moment to think about the things that are most important to you. Once you identify them, you can give gratitude for them as often as you want.

When either of us has a bad thought or one that causes our energy to flow in a direction we don't want it to, we turn to an affirmation card we carry with us that says, *"Thank you, God, for showing me that I'm focusing on and creating what I do not want in my life right now. Please help me redirect my focus to what I do want."*

Once you know what you want and can give gratitude for it, it's time to change your vibration. Maintaining a high vibration is so important, and to do that, we have to frequently check our vibe in order to know where we are at all times. You can measure your vibration on a scale from one to ten, just like you can with the levels of hair. For example, if you drop below an eight on the vibration scale, you can expect to be less productive than you would be if you were vibing at a nine or ten. Energy is also contagious. To put this into perspective, it may interest you to know that the vibration of fun, joy, and laughter is actually on the same frequency as money!

Six-Figure Stylists are confident, so if that's who you want to become, we recommend setting aside ten minutes of each day to focus on affirmations that build your confidence and improve your posture. Try doing this in the car or in the mirror while you get ready. Daily affirmations centered on what you know to be true about yourself, or maybe even what you would like to be true in the near future, will help you continue or start to believe them and build your confidence. Later in this book, we will include some affirmations that you can borrow until you create your own. The more we do things, the more we gain confidence in them. When you learned to ride a bike, you might not have gotten the hang of it right away. Then, as you kept practicing, you probably got better and gained confidence from your progress. The next thing you know, you could ride with your eyes closed and without hands. Build those confidence muscles!

You can plan your personal life much like you would your professional one in order to help you achieve a higher vibration and work and live with intention. We do this by scheduling our day around our nine highest values. Yours may be different from ours, but if you have a hard time figuring yours out, feel free to use some of these examples.

Our values revolve around spiritual connection, being family-focused, being vibrantly healthy, being financially free, happiness, fun, joy, love, appreciation, kindness toward ourselves and others, making a difference, personal growth, and being neat and organized. Each evening, we both take about fifteen minutes to plan out the next day, from when we wake up to when we go to sleep. This isn't to be confused with a to-do list; each activity relates to one or more of our highest values. Activities that involve more than one value are the best because they take us to higher vibrations. For example, going to the gym benefits your health, brings joy, and shows your love and appreciation for yourself. What you choose to listen to during this time can add even more value to the mix. Praise and worship music, devotionals, or even the Bible can nurture one's spiritual health. This one example touched on five of the nine values, and this is why exercise is nonnegotiable for Lacey.

Did you know that giving gratitude within the first fifteen minutes of waking up can dramatically boost your immune system? (Source: heart.org.) That's right! At the end of this chapter, Lacey will outline her gratitude process so you can reference it while building your own. Kylie, for example, has a thirty-minute commute to work every day, so she usually expresses her gratitude while she's in the car.

Think about how you engage with your clients and how your positive or negative energy may affect that visit for both the guest and you—like energy attracts like energy. If your vibe is at a higher level while you're in the salon, do you think your guests will be inclined to spend more time and, therefore, more money with you? Of course!

Check your vibration before walking into the salon or clear your energy between clients. If the weather is nice, take two or three minutes outside if you need to really clear up your energy. Try putting on an upbeat song and dancing around or doing jumping jacks. This works like a charm! Check-in with yourself throughout the day or if you feel off. Did you do your morning gratitude routine? Are you grateful for the clients sitting in your chairs? Are you grateful to be at work? Or, do you feel like you'd rather be anywhere else and all your walk-ins are nuisances? Our thought processes directly affect our success.

We recommend hiring a life coach, but if you're not sure or not in a financial place to do so, try checking in with a salon buddy and establishing accountability partners. Professional sports teams have a coach, as do actors and singers. You get the point. A coach is someone who can help you hone in on your skills. A mentor is someone who helps you on the emotional side of things. In this case, they would focus on the emotional side of your business because there's emotion behind everything, even in the professional world. Mentors can help us spot things like mental blocks and guide us in a better direction.

Lacey's daily gratitude practice includes about five minutes of freely flowing gratitude the moment she awakens, usually with her eyes still closed. What are you grateful for? Her stream of consciousness at this point in the practice usually sounds something like, *"Thank you, God, for a new day full of favor and abundance. Thank you for giving me rest and readying my soul to greet this day you have created for me. Thank you for guiding every thought in my mind and every word from my mouth. Thank you for your wisdom and knowledge. Thank you, God, for going before me and behind me, leading me in my footsteps. I'm so grateful for this warm bed and to wake up to my vibrantly healthy family."*

She then spends another five minutes expressing gratitude for her nine highest values.

- I'm so grateful for my spiritual connection.
- I'm so grateful to be family-focused.
- I'm so grateful to be vibrantly healthy.
- I'm so grateful to have spare time and financial freedom.
- I'm so grateful to be happy and full of fun, joy, and laughter.
- I'm so grateful to have love, appreciation, and kindness for myself and others.
- I'm so grateful to be able to make a difference in the world.
- I'm so grateful to be constantly growing as a person.
- I'm so grateful to be neat and organized.

She spends five more minutes expressing gratitude for her healthy body and the miracle of the human body in general. She visualizes and moves each part as she gives gratitude. It's easy to feel grateful on this front if you know someone who has been physically ill or struggled with a certain injury or ailment.

- I'm so grateful for the miracle of the human body.
- I'm so grateful for my ten vibrantly healthy toes.

- I'm so grateful for my vibrantly healthy feet and ankles.
- I'm so grateful for my vibrantly healthy legs.
- I'm so grateful for my vibrantly healthy knees.
- I'm so grateful for my vibrantly healthy hips.
- I'm so grateful that all of my bones are vibrantly healthy.
- I'm so grateful that all of my muscles are vibrantly healthy.
- I'm so grateful that all of my joints are vibrantly healthy.
- I'm so grateful that all of my glands are vibrantly healthy.
- I'm so grateful that all of my lymph nodes are vibrantly healthy.
- I'm so grateful that my blood is vibrantly healthy.
- I'm so grateful that all of my organs are vibrantly healthy. (Lacey typically lists the organs individually, but that's up to you.)
- I'm so grateful for my vibrantly healthy breasts and nipples.
- I'm so grateful for my vibrantly healthy shoulders and elbows.
- I'm so grateful for my vibrantly healthy wrists and hands.
- I'm so very grateful for my ten vibrantly healthy fingers.
- I'm so grateful for my vibrantly healthy spine.
- I'm so grateful for my vibrantly healthy throat, mouth, and tongue.
- I'm so grateful for my vibrantly healthy nose and sinuses.
- I'm so grateful for my vibrantly healthy eyes.
- I'm so grateful for my vibrantly healthy ears.
- I'm so grateful for my vibrantly healthy mind.
- I'm so grateful for my vibrantly healthy hair follicles and my thick, luscious hair.
- I'm so grateful for my vibrantly healthy immune system.
- I'm so grateful that every cell in my body is vibrantly healthy.

Next, she takes three to five minutes to make statements starting with "I choose to be," "I am," or "it feels so good to be" for each one of her nine highest values, like the following sentence. "I choose to be spiritually connected. I am spiritually connected. It feels so good to be spiritually connected." Then, she raises one or both of her arms and brings them down with a big "Yes!" Try to hold that feeling for seventeen seconds before moving on to the next value on your list.

After each value is addressed, she takes a few minutes to write everything she is grateful for in a gratitude journal or on a gratitude chart. This typically includes the things she's praying for, but she gives gratitude for them as if the matters have already been resolved.

Six-Figure Stylist Takeaways:

- Be specific about what you want.
- Visualize it and hang onto the feelings you associate with it for seventeen seconds.
- Have faith that it will be done.
- Know to measure where you are on the vibration scale.
- Express what you are grateful for.
- Identify action steps you can take to improve your life right now.

"Bonus Resources" to enhance your experience.

- A mini-course to discover your nine highest values
- Daily gratitude practice guide
- Carry along Gratitude Card

PLEASE SCAN THE QR CODE TO ACCESS:

Resources:

- *The Magic and Asking High Vibrational Questions* by Bill Mayer
- *Little Voice Mastery: How to Win the War Between Your Ears in 30 Seconds or Less and Have an Extraordinary Life!* by Blair Singer.

CHAPTER 2

BECOME A MAGNETIC MONEY MACHINE

Now that we have our thought process figured out, let's work on becoming a magnetic money machine. The first thing you need to address is the relationship between your current numbers and your future goals.

> *"To begin with the end in mind means to start with a clear understanding of your destination. It means to know where you're going so that you better understand where you are now and so that the steps you take are always in the right direction."*
> – Stephen R. Covey

Six-Figure Stylists have goals. Many people don't have a firm grasp on their current numbers, their future goals, or even what money they need to live. Let's work backward. After we come up with our total expenses for the month, we can break that down by the costs we incur throughout a typical week and then the daily charges. Don't forget tips and retail purchases. It's all real money! Kylie has had stylists at her salon company who were able to pay their car payments with what they earned in retail commission alone.

Let's start with your monthly expenses. The following list includes some things to think about. You may have more items in your final list, or you may have less.

- Car payment
- Car insurance
- Car maintenance
- Electricity
- Gas
- Water
- Trash pickup
- Other utilities (Wi-Fi, cable, etc.)
- Subscriptions (Amazon Prime, Netflix, etc.)
- Health insurance
- Life insurance
- Retirement
- Savings
- Fuel
- Groceries
- Rent or mortgage
- Gym membership
- Self-care
- Kids' sports programs
- Clothing
- Entertainment
- Habits (alcohol, cigarettes, vaping, etc.)

When you're done, add it all up. If it's $5,000 per month, for example, then you need to be grossing at least $10,000 to pay your bills. If you work a five-day workweek, four weeks per month, your weekly service dollar goal is $2,500, and the daily service goal is $500.

How many guests will it take you to reach your daily goal? To know this, you need to know how much you typically earn on an average ticket. Take the monthly service total and divide it by the number of guests you seat in your chair; this is your average ticket. So, if I did $10,000 in services and saw ninety guests that month, then my average ticket would be $111.11.

$$\text{Average Ticket} = \frac{\$10{,}000}{90} = \$111.11$$

If you have fewer guests, you need to work on increasing your service-to-client ratio (which means doing more services on the same number of guests) and/or add more high-ticket offerings to your list of services.

Now, let's think about the income that you desire. What services can we include in your repertoire to add to your bottom line? Six-Figure Stylists have strategies for increasing revenue, like offering innovative salon services. Research what's trending and the latest styles. Hair extensions, hair pieces, and toppers are all part of a multibillion-dollar industry. Collagen is a multibillion-dollar industry. You have to be innovative, and you can't just do the same thing over and over and expect a different outcome. That's the definition of insanity. Keep growing, researching, and striving for better outcomes. We're here to help you with that! One of the fantastic opportunities we have as stylists is the ability to take charge of how much money we make. Make authentic offerings to your guests, and don't be afraid to ask (i.e., ask if they have the time to do the service you are suggesting. Give them the details—what it does, why they need it, what the process looks like, how long it takes, and how much it costs). Hot tip: the one who speaks first loses. So ask them if they want the service and give them time to think about it. If we get in our own heads, we can often talk them out of it. So stand back and wait for their response. Realize that *no* can be a beautiful word and that sometimes it just means *not right now*.

What's going to bring in the most money for your time? Is it doing kids' haircuts all day? We don't think so. So, consider offering some high-ticket items, even if it means you have to earn a new certification or become a specialist. Independent salon professionals and salon owners make a higher profit margin on products they can sell compared to actual services, but commissioned service providers earn the majority of their income on those services. Think of it this way: if you could make about $1,000 doing hair extensions in an hour or two versus making roughly $100 on something less expensive while serving two or three clients, which would you prioritize?

Six-Figure Stylists have high client retention and book their regulars' next appointments before they leave the salon. Your pre-book percentage should be at least 70%. If not, you're operating at a low retention rate and will be forever chasing down new clients. Booking a client's next appointment before they leave is your insurance policy for future income. If you don't employ this strategy, there's always a chance that they won't come back, or it could be months before they do. So, if you want to be able to count on the amount of money you're going to make in the next month or two, then you need to get them on your books right away. One way you can do this is by setting up a consultation. You want to ensure the guest can afford the time and financial commitment to maintain the look they're asking for, whether it's color, extensions, or length maintenance. You want them to know that your top priority is protecting the integrity of their hair and that you want them to love their style. This means you'll need to earn their trust as their confident salon professional.

Six-Figure Stylists tell their clients when they need to come back for touch-ups and to maintain the best results for their hair. Don't ask your guests if or when they want to come back and see you. And whatever you do, do not ask if they want to just call and book their next appointment later. You're the professional, so tell them during the consultation what the ideal schedule of the next appointments will look like for their particular style needs. Then, at the end of the visit, ask them which days and times work best for them. It is imperative to protect your future revenue and to be able to plan who you have in your chair month to month, how much time to set aside for them, and how much you'll make for your services. This also ensures that the client's look stays relevant and that they can meet with you in the best time frame for both of your schedules. A busy stylist may even book clients six months to a year out and several appointments at a time per guest. Otherwise, they might have to take off from work just like they would for a doctor's appointment. Image is everything; the better you look, the better you feel.

In 2006, at the age of twenty-five, Lacey opened a high-end salon and spa. She had absolutely no idea what she was doing. Thankfully, she'd invested in a good coach who helped her along the way. She thought this would be unaffordable, but as it turned out, she couldn't afford not to have the extra guidance. The salon was an absolutely gorgeous place with all the bells and whistles (too many, according to our coach), and tons of new guests came through the door from the get-go. The only problem was that she couldn't seem to retain any of them as regulars. They weren't scheduling their next appointments before they left. The salon's pre-book percentage was less than 50%, which meant that about half of the money she was currently banking on wasn't planning to come back. She even sent out handwritten thank-you notes (which we still recommend), but even that didn't always work. When your business is new, it is vital that you have this kind of system in place because you're going to get more new business in the beginning. You can't lose the momentum because even if you make a good first impression, if you haven't gotten the clients to commit to future visits, you can kiss them and their money goodbye. Make them feel at home with you, your skills, and the salon environment. Create an experience they will never forget and will want to share with their friends.

Lacey had to bring in Randy Kunkel, the owner of multiple salons and cofounder of KRS Consulting Group, to help get her pre-book rates up and to see what she could do to ensure the future of the business. She found herself awake night after night, running reports and calculating what was on the books to make sure she'd earn enough to pay her employees and the bills; she was lucky if she got to pay herself on time within those first six months. Kunkel gave her some simple yet brilliant advice. "Lacey! Quit asking and start telling!" In one month, the salon's pre-book percentage soared to 70%. The month after that, it was up to 75%! It continued in this manner as long as everyone was trained and confident, including the front desk staff. To this day, all of her guests book multiple appointments unless they are unable to.

To find your pre-book percentage, divide the total number of guests who pre-booked their appointments by the total number of salon guests. If thirty-six clients pre-booked, but there were fifty-nine total clients, your pre-book percentage is 61%.

$$\textbf{Pre-Book Percentage} = \left(\tfrac{36}{59}\right) \times 100 \approx 61\%$$

Let's look at the daily routines of successful salon professionals. Six-Figure Stylists show up at least fifteen minutes early in order to plan for success. We like to say that being on time is being late. This doesn't mean running through the door like your hair's on fire, and your first guest shouldn't beat you there. This isn't a good look because they'll know you've had zero time to prepare for your day, much less their specific appointment. Get settled in and see who you have coming in that day and how much time you have in between each guest. Do you have any free periods in which you could take another client or add on additional services for the ones you have scheduled? Take the time to jot down which services you can offer during their consultations.

If they are returning guests, you could also double-check which products they have purchased in the past and figure out when they might be running low on those. Maybe they've purchased products to help straighten their hair, but you know that their hair is naturally wavy and that they haven't bought anything lately that could open the door for you to teach them another way to style their hair or recommend other products or a tool. It's all about adding value to the experience.

You could also plan to do a tutorial for your social media platforms. Invest in a tripod and a ring light you can set up right at your station and plan out how to capture and utilize the content. If you know that you're doing hair extensions or corrective color that day, you want to plan ahead in order to capture both the before and the after content.

> *"Success isn't a series of hacks. There's no secret strategy everyone else knows that you don't know. Success is about showing up every single day and putting in the work. On the good days, and the bad days."*
> –Brandon Bornancin

When Lacey learned to start implementing these daily practices, everything changed! Her service sales doubled right away, and her retail sales increased more than ever before—as did her service-to-client ratio, average ticket totals, referrals, and everything! Everything seemed to come together because she put intention behind everything she did.

Kylie and her associate, Jordan, made their daily planning ritual into a fun game. They would look at what services they could add on if time allowed and what retail each specific client would need in order to maintain their look. One day, they challenged themselves to include as much intention behind their usual planning strategy as possible and wound up having a record-breaking day of $786 in retail sales! You've got to measure what you treasure. We have invested countless hours and countless dollars in learning these skills and being able to work seamlessly. If you do two hundred services in a month for ninety guests in a month, then divide the number of services by the number of guests, you get a service-to-client ratio of 2.22.

$$\text{Service-to-Client Ratio} = \frac{200}{90} \approx 2.22$$

Frankly, two services per guest isn't enough. It's smarter to do more services for those you already have in your chair.

Now, this doesn't mean you have to turn into a sleazy salesperson. We would never sell a guest something they didn't need just for the transaction. There are plenty of people who do things like this and take advantage of others, but that's not what we're about. We want to emphasize authentic offerings on retail, services, and service add-ons. That's what it means to truly serve a guest from the heart. Our job is to tell them what we use and why we chose that for their hair. We go above and beyond when we teach them how to use it themselves. We don't allow them to leave and run to Target or Ulta and let a shelf pick out something for their hair. As beauty professionals, we know better than a shelf.

For example, Kylie had a guest book a consultation for a hair topper. During the consultation, she determined that a topper wasn't the best solution for this guest because their hair loss was fairly extensive; she would be better off with a wig. That being said, Kylie keeps hair toppers on hand. Why? Because when someone wants something, they want it right away—especially when it comes to hair loss solutions—and if you don't have it, you can't sell it. She gave the client her honest opinion and sent her home with some resources on wigs. To her associate, she later said, "I could have sold her a topper, easy. The client was desperate. But I know that it wouldn't have been the best long-term solution for her, as she'll continue to lose hair. I could've made a $1,000 sale, but not with integrity."

Six-Figure Stylists measure the lifetime value of a salon guest. Earlier in the chapter, we taught you how to figure out your average ticket, which can help us calculate what our average guest spends. For example, if our average guest spends $2,000 with us each year and we've served them for twenty years, the lifetime value of the client is $40,000.

$$\text{Lifetime Value (LTV)} = \$2,000 \times 20 = \$40,000$$

So, we really need to keep that client happy with us. And if you think about it, that annual rate is not a lot of money to spend in the salon. Some people spend $2,000 every couple of months. So, it really depends on each stylist and guest. Therefore, stylists need to be able to figure out the lifetime value of each guest and how it affects their income. Doing so puts things in perspective and also allows a closer look at the overall health of one's business.

We've talked about some things that can help transform you into a magnetic money machine. Now, let's talk about what doesn't. A lack of confidence is probably one of the main reasons stylists don't achieve their financial goals. They either don't believe in the story they're telling themselves, or they don't believe in what they're selling. Sometimes, you have to fake it until you make it. We recommend borrowing someone else's words to bolster you until you find your own.

"You sometimes lose by taking risks; you always lose by holding back."
–Rachel Wolchin

Repetition can be a wonderful confidence booster. The more you do something, the more often you see a certain result, thus boosting your confidence.

Another thing that doesn't help is if you find yourself constantly rescheduling or calling in sick. People value their self-care time, and they sometimes restructure their schedule around their appointments with you. If you find yourself getting into this habit, we recommend correcting it as soon as possible. If not, you may find yourself losing clients faster than you can attract them.

Six-Figure Stylists know their worth. They know that discounting a service won't necessarily do you or your business any favors. Discounting services can reflect low self-worth and, therefore, low vibes. We have seen this happen all over the country in various salons, including our own. We encourage you to take a look at your last year's budget and earnings and determine how much money you gave away in discounts. Here's an example of how you might break it down.

If Mary works five days a week and doesn't charge for extra color treatment for one guest each day (which isn't that uncommon) but should charge an additional $30 for this add-on service according to salon policy, that's $150 lost every week, or about $7,500 for the year. That translates to about $3,750 that Mary loses from her own pay. If five salon employees do this, that's $37,500 lost for the entire year's revenue. The day-to-day details can add up to big differences.

- **Daily Loss Per Guest:** Daily Loss $= 1 \times \$30 = \$30$
- **Weekly Loss:** Weekly Loss $= \$30 \times 5 = \$150$
- **Annual Loss for Mary:** Annual Loss for Mary $= \$150 \times 50 = \$7,500$ (assuming 50 work weeks per year)
- **Mary's Personal Annual Loss:** Mary's Personal Annual Loss $= \$7,500 \div 2 = \$3,750$
- **Total Annual Loss for Salon with Five Employees:** Total Annual Loss for Salon $= \$3,750 \times 5 = \$18,750$

When we first became salon owners, we quickly realized that we had to put a cap on discounts. When we discovered the amount of discounts that were being given, we felt like we had been robbed. If the salon owner paid for the color materials, and then that product was used but not charged for, the owner is the one who loses money. On top of that, the stylist loses money that could have been used to pay bills, put food on the table, and make investments for the future. It's tempting to give guests a break when we know every detail about them, especially if they're experiencing financial hardships, but you have to remember that how they choose to spend their money is up to them and none of our business. Our job is to recommend services and products based on their needs or wants, give them as accurate a cost estimate as we can, and let them make their own decisions. It's no different than going to the store for five items but realizing that your budget is limited to covering only three.

Sometimes, without even realizing it, a stylist can adopt a bad attitude toward a guest because they are not as valuable as others. They can start to feel as if the guest owes them something, or may even decide to phone it in on their services since the rate they'll earn isn't stellar. Sometimes, the guest knows they are getting a break, but sometimes, they may not even be aware. What happens if you need to stay late for a discounted guest? Are you as eager to do your best work? Or would you be inclined to have a surly attitude about it? Take a moment before you go on and jot down how many people—if any—you give discounts to. Why do you give them the discounts? What feelings do you have toward them?

Last but not least, to become a magnetic money machine, we have to know what the heck we are going to do with those earnings if we do get them. Remember to begin with the end in mind. Look up Regan Hillyer's YouTube videos; her teachings are phenomenal. She suggests we start by visualizing what it would be like to have this money, then assess why we want it in the first place. Allow yourself to feel as if you've already gotten it. Next, we've got to take action with the choices we make every day to acquire that sweet moolah. According to Regan, you have to have the capacity to hold the energy in order to acquire it. She challenges us to take a look at our relationship with money.

Keep reading for a daily checklist you can use to set yourself up for success and become a magnetic money machine.

Six-Figure Stylist Takeaways:

- Find your pre-book percentage.
- Calculate your average ticket: total service sales amount divided by the number of guests.
- Establish your monthly service sales goal.
- What conversations do you need to have about salon discounts?
- Categorize your clients based on their annual and lifetime values.

Daily Success Checklist:

- Morning gratitude practice
- Health and vibe check
- Arrive early
- Plan out the day
- Change shoes
- Enjoy some high-vibe food
- Plan content for social media and marketing
- Daily social post
- Set up social software if needed
- Check-in with an accountability partner or salon mentor
- Check for all the products and tools needed for the day's guests
- Confirm tomorrow's appointments
- Complete follow-ups
- Recharge batteries (meditate, pray, work out, or do something just for themselves). Most stylists we know end up sitting in their cars with no music. They don't really want to speak to anyone because they have been hyperstimulated all day and have nothing left.

"Bonus Resources" to enhance your experience.

- Tracking journal
- Six-Figure goal setting
- Pre-booking scripts

PLEASE SCAN THE QR CODE TO ACCESS:

Resources:

- *Whatever It Takes: Master the Habits to Transform Your Business, Relationships, and Life* by Brandon Bornancin
- *Rich Dad Poor Dad: What the Rich Teach Their Kids About Money That the Poor and Middle Class Do Not!* by Robert T. Kiyosaki
- Regan Hillyer's YouTube channel

CHAPTER 3

ESSENTIAL ELEMENTS OF BUILDING YOUR BEAUTY BRAND

Six-Figure Stylists know who they are as people. It might sound kind of weird, but people buy people. Or think of it as they're buying you as their beauty professional or buying into your brand.

> *"People don't buy from people who don't give a sh** about them. People buy from people who are committed to maximizing their success."*
> –Brandon Bornancin.

So, refer back to your core values and figure out what you stand for. Who are you? What are your hobbies and interests? That's all part of your brand. You're building more than just a beauty business or a list of regular clients. You're building the business of your dreams based on what is authentically you. Most people spend the majority of their lives working and sleeping. Make sure you love what you do the most during your waking hours!

When you find yourself, people will find you, and you will eventually establish your tribe. A recent study has shown that authenticity is the highest vibration that the body puts out. (Source: ninaamir.com.) If you're genuine in your true self, you're that much more likely to be successful. In order to do that, you have to know who you are as a brand. Are you crunchy, organic, or vegan? Do you like to work out? Are you spiritual? Who are you, both as an individual and as a beauty professional? Everything about you and the work you showcase needs to be in line with your brand.

Look at companies like Apple. It's never about the device; they sell happiness. The marketing campaigns are about the memories people can capture on the iPhone or the life they can live because they can work from anywhere thanks to this phone. The tech comes as a secondary message to the emotional response.

Lacey shares some hair photos on her social media, mostly hair extensions and transformations. If you follow her, you will notice content that also identifies her as a Christian wife and mom. She's passionate about wellness and a plant-based, holistic lifestyle. She shares American-made, nontoxic products that she believes in, as well as ways others can save or earn money. She shares programs for beauty businesses alongside tips to help people with their spiritual, financial, and physical well-being.

Marketing can be outsourced if necessary, or you can hire a branding strategist. We have both done this, and we highly recommend it. Burch Branding, for instance, can manage a business's content if nobody on staff has the time or desire to run the social media accounts. Talk about taking a load off! They also have consulting services to help establish a brand online and then hand it back over to the business to manage. There are pain points for everyone, so if you're feeling burnt out, consider outsourcing tasks you don't necessarily need to keep on your plate. There's a resource for you at the end of this chapter if this is something you'd like to look into further.

It used to take so much money and so many resources to get a new client in the door. And now, what's the first thing we go to when we want to learn more about somebody or a business? We look them up online. We look at their social media accounts or their website. What does your social window and digital footprint say about who you are? What kind of hair do you have? What do you like to do? Do you often use bold colors? Do you specialize in hair extensions? Are you all business? Do you do men's cuts? What is it that attracts people to you? These days, people want to know and see you, not just your work. If you want more extension business, wear extensions in a few photos you post. Show me a stylist who doesn't color their hair, and we'll show you a stylist who doesn't have many guests requesting color services. Show me a stylist who doesn't use products on their own hair, and we'll show you a stylist who doesn't sell many products. Be your own influencer. Put out what you want to attract.

During social media training sessions that Lacey completed to help other salons as well as her own business, she discovered that, as an artist, she had to brand herself. How would salons know to book her if she wasn't posting about what she had to offer? The same goes for potential salon guests. If you do multiple things, sometimes they can fall under the same umbrella. But, if they don't make sense in relation to your brand, you may choose to have multiple brands, all with their own social media accounts. Have you considered monetizing your Pinterest? Currently, TikTok can help certain types of businesses and individuals get way more exposure than all the other available platforms combined.

Be a walking billboard. We've both built up our hair clientele through waitressing and bartending. This was before social media, but in-person networking is still relevant today. When you put yourself in front of the public in any capacity, you have a built-in audience and a reason to talk to people. We tried anything from working a different or second job to actively campaigning for new clients. We visited businesses with our brochures, business cards, pens, and other promotional items. We both joined different organizations and networked. We'll talk more about these strategies in a bit, but now we have social media that we can leverage, and there are some really smart strategies out there that can encourage effective engagement and growth.

For example, we both use AI software called MyGeniusLeads, which maximizes one's algorithm. This sends out messages, engages with other accounts, and sends out friend requests on behalf of the user. You can share stories and engage with people who see or like your story. If you see content on somebody's page that you like but don't have the money to hire somebody to do something similar for yours, this software can help you create similar posts without compromising your unique online identity or that of the account you drew inspiration from. This software can even send emails and texts!

For way too long, we spent way too much time on our phones. We started to feel guilty about engaging on our phones 24/7. How much time do you spend on your devices? And how much of that time was intentionally spent online?

Before we found MyGeniusLeads, we used to always see the same few accounts on our feeds with comments from the same people. Where was everyone else? We didn't understand the algorithm. Every day, we would intend to send " birthday messages" to our closest contacts but never remembered to do so on time. That was actually the first tool Lacey utilized. She scheduled it to go out three days prior to someone's birthday when they anticipated it and not the day of, because the messages were more likely to get lost among the others. We couldn't believe the change we saw in the amount of engagement our account garnered, and all by just asking a small question and wishing others a happy early birthday! This allowed us to engage in messenger and place each conversation in a customer relationship management (CRM) system in order to see our warm market.

All of a sudden, new accounts appeared in our feed and left comments on our posts and stories. Once she started organizing accounts in our CRM, she discovered that this tool made it possible for us to send out between twenty-five and fifty messages at one time. This, in turn, helped us start maximizing the algorithm while spending less time on social media. We let the software start conversations for us so we could pick it up later when we had time. No more endless scrolling: when we identified who was in our warm market, we could go directly to their pages and engage with purpose. We utilized the disconnector tool in relation to old, inactive accounts or people who weren't engaging with us. This made room for new friends; we learned how to automatically connect with those we had things in common with so the software could work while we went to the gym or spent time with family. Talk about working smarter, not harder!

If you're active in groups as well as your local community, you can connect with potential salon clients or someone who'd like to purchase products you sell—not only in the salon but online as well—maximizing your earning potential alongside the sales bot that helps close sales when you're otherwise occupied.

When we're behind the chair, we are not glued to our phones. If we're using our phones behind the chair, it needs to be limited to taking before and after photos or shooting content videos. We're not on social media unless it's a slow day because we definitely don't want to be caught in a "doomscroll" while on the clock. Using a tool like the one we rely on can be set up to work independently and efficiently to avoid this. Lacey sets it up in the morning before she leaves the house. Then she goes to work or wherever else she needs to go—like the gym or dropping her daughter off at school—and she can pick up the conversation later. It is her authentic message, but this tool really helps her strategize and make her account's engagement so much more effective. Plus, it gave us time back. As stylists, we feel like anybody who's marketing themselves or selling anything online should check it out.

So, what is your marketing plan? Write out the key components of what you are doing now. As you continue through this chapter, we encourage you to highlight or make notes of things you might add to benefit your current strategy.

Are you posting about any promotions you've tried? It's important to have a service offering or product promotion every six to eight weeks because this is the typical salon guest schedule. Offering regular product promotions creates more of a shopping environment and great opportunities to change up the displays showcasing the items you carry in the salon. Even if there aren't a lot of new products to speak of, if the area looks different, it creates curiosity and invites people to look around. It's kind of like rearranging furniture at home; if things never change, they can look the same even when you get new items.

Having regular service promotions gives salon guests the ability to try out something they might not have, as well as the opportunity to pre-book for that service. Think of services you'd like to do more of, or maybe there's something new you'd like to introduce to your regulars. Years ago, when Lacey was new to using Redken, they came out with the Redken Chemistry system, an innovative conditioning treatment. They called them Chem Shots. Her guests were not used to getting these kinds of treatments, and Lacey didn't offer them until these came into play. She learned that she could customize the treatment for each individual's needs and rebalance their hair's pH levels before or after a chemical service. To top it all off, the effect would last twenty-one days. She immediately ran a promotion, and each color appointment booked during that eight-week promotion received a free conditioning treatment. Every client who received a free treatment still loves them and gets them today. They saw the value in the treatment and can even feel when it begins to wear off. What this small change in add-on services did for Lacey's bottom line was life-changing! That year, she gave herself a $10,000 raise thanks to that treatment alone.

Another time, an educator came to her salon and taught the stylists how to perform a chemical peel at the shampoo bowl. They each did a peel on a fellow stylist so everyone could experience it, and all the stylists loved it. The peel only takes about five minutes from start to finish and only costs $60 to have done. A special promotion was a great way to introduce it to the salon, and it, too, was met with a warm welcome. And just one peel a day at this price adds up to an extra $7,500 each year for the beauty professional!

Is there an amazing service that you offer, but hardly anyone gets or knows about it? Jot down a few things you love to have done yourself, and set an intention to promote that service to your clients.

You can have pre-booking contests in your salon for six to eight weeks at a time, where each guest and service provider gets their name put in a drawing for a special prize for each appointment booked. Or you can hold a referral contest, in which each person who refers a new client and the service provider is entered to win. Just make sure it's a prize that's worth everyone's while! Ask your staff what would motivate them. You could get all kinds of responses: cash, a big TV, Amazon gift cards, the newest Apple product, a gas grill, or, if you're feeling generous, a trip. It's especially helpful if you post the prize at the front of the salon for everyone to see as soon as they walk in. We promise you they will ask about it and want to get involved. Look at your numbers and see what type of promotion would be most beneficial to your salon as a whole. If your business needs more guests, try the referral contest. Is there a particular month in which business is always slower? Be strategic and plan a pre-booking contest leading up to that period.

In the beginning, Kylie was attending three networking events per week to shout from the rooftops who she was and what her salon company was all about. Styling hair is a very personal experience, so it makes sense that we would want to promote ourselves by making real human connections. Was it scary to be in a room of eighty people all passing around a microphone and talking about themselves? Hell yes! However, it didn't deter her from her pursuit of success. What was amazing were the relationships developed between these people and how the group was industry-specific. Once you were in, no other person from your profession could join; everyone referred each other. We were also both members of Business Networking International (BNI), where we met once a week with other entrepreneurs in the area to get exposure. We gained some of our best clients from these meetings.

Six-Figure Stylists utilize a referral program. Referrals are our favorite type of new guest at the salon. It's our favorite kind of marketing because other people advertise for us. When we asked for referrals back in the day, we'd give out a few cards to each client and ask them to send in their friends to see us. This really wasn't very effective because the business cards just ended up in the trash can. So, we recommend getting really specific regarding how you ask for referrals. Now, we use a 20/20 referral program. This is when we have somebody who sends in a referral for a color service or more, and we give both the person who referred and the person being referred twenty bucks off. That way, everyone gets a "thank you" for bringing us new business.

To determine how we should communicate this offer, we categorize our clients. We have our top five clients, but you might want to use a different system. Who are your clients with the highest tickets on average? That is who you are most likely to ask for referrals. When you ask, be specific. Maybe I have a regular named Tina, and I know she has friends who, chances are, will want to spend like she wants to spend when it comes to their haircare. There's a certain percentage of the population that actually wants to spend more on such things than they do. So, you find the people you enjoy doing services for, and who you enjoy spending time with, then you ask them about who they spend most of their time with. From there, work your way up to asking them to either put you in direct contact with them or introduce you to them and offer them a free consultation. Send a digital business card; if you don't have a digital business card, you can provide your contact information or have them send your Instagram or preferred social media profile details so they can see your work beforehand. Employ a consistent referral program that benefits your current clients and makes you look like the successful, in-demand stylist you are.

Six-Figure Stylists also market themselves. A great resource for this is Real Beauty Bosses, an online business growth and support system for beauty professionals. Kylie learned firsthand that their strategic marketing efforts yield a constant flow of new traffic and salon sales. Real Beauty Bosses ran targeted ads and, in six months, added about $64,000 from advertising hair extensions. Join your town's chamber of commerce or a gym. Go to classes and events; you could even host events at your salon. Recently, we hosted a hair topper event in a retirement community. Not only did we get the opportunity to serve new guests and help them regain their confidence, but we established new relationships and generated $9,000 in just a few hours.

Charity fundraiser events are a great way to give back and network. A lot of times, we'll have people walk in and ask for donation baskets for these kinds of events, but don't just donate a basket. Be a part of that event and your local community. We were able to do this with a local children's home that incorporated a fashion show. Once, Lacey worked at a salon that did a Zumbathon to raise money for the American Heart Association. Each participant raised money in the salon and turned in the entry fee for the Zumbathon. Local businesses donated baskets, prizes, and gift cards for a silent auction, and all the proceeds went to the cause. This was a win-win because Lacey got to exercise, have fun, meet new people (potential clients), and most importantly, raise money for a good cause.

Do photoshoots. Get in touch with a photography student or even a local photographer who also wants to build their business. Get in with local or possibly more far-reaching magazines. When Lacey owned her salon and spa, she linked up with a local magazine and paid to do hair for an editorial. At first, this wasn't her favorite type of advertising because she felt like she should be getting paid for her services and talent. But, having her work published in a magazine was way more beneficial for her career than a full, one-page spread that a business would typically have to pay for. She also met the models and got to know the designers. This led to her being involved in more editorial work and even a local fashion week. She had the relationships and found herself in the right circles to learn about every event that she would want to be a part of. This also opened the door to fashion week stylings in other states and helped when she auditioned to become a certified "Redken Artist." Big companies always want to see what you've done and where your work has been published.

If this interests you, think about who you want to model for you. Hair is our canvas, and you probably already have someone who frequently occupies your chair who could be a model or who would know of someone who does.

So, if your overall vibe is Gucci, maybe you could purchase some Gucci clothes and accessories for your model to wear and then send the finished photos off to Gucci for potential opportunities. After all, who knows more about fashion than a hairstylist? We can always be spotted in a crowd because we have style. We follow fashion trends because it all flows together.

See if there's a fashion week that you can get involved with, or maybe you can start one in your area. There are fashion societies, like Fashion Group International, and even some different ways to get involved with New York Fashion Week (NYFW). Most beauty professionals don't start out getting asked to go to NYFW, and most that do have to pay to go; think of it as part of your advertising budget. The photos and videos of you and your work may get published in countless places, and you can take incredible pictures on your own phone for your social media. Once you're there, make an impression. Sometimes, people get asked to be a lead, but if you aren't, you can at least inquire about what it takes to be asked to be a lead, who to contact, and how to get paid to go. Don't forget, it all starts with a thought, followed by visualization. If styling at a fashion week is a goal of yours, make sure you visualize yourself doing just that and then take action. That's exactly how Lacey wound up getting a phone call to work backstage at NYFW.

There are various running clubs like She RUNS This Town. If you're a runner, team up with your favorite charity or raise money through a marathon, half marathon, or even a 5K. It's the absolute best when you can help out with a cause that you genuinely care about. And when you do those things, you have to blast it on your social media channels. Get others involved and make it fun while you're making an impact and staying in shape! When you're excited about things, other people feel that vibration, and they get excited, too. If you're not confident enough to go for it or tell people that you're doing it, then you're not going to be that successful. Become obsessed with what you're doing and do it all on purpose.

Gain momentum. Don't be afraid to pay for marketing if you can afford it. While we're talking about marketing, we want to bring up something that has been taboo for quite some time in our industry: affiliate marketing. Some of the most successful entrepreneurs in the world—Tony Robbins, Grant Cardone, and even Kevin O'Leary—all engage in affiliate or network marketing.

> "The Network Marketing industry offers a ready-made business system to anyone wanting to take control of their financial future."
> –Robert T. Kiyosaki

We are huge fans of affiliate and network marketing, as well as multiple profit streams. I'm sure we've all heard the saying about not putting your eggs in one basket. When we rely solely on income that comes from behind the chair, that's exactly what we're doing. The average millionaire has roughly seven income streams.

> "If you don't find a way to make money while you sleep, you will work until you die."
> –Warren Buffett

We highly recommend finding things that you believe in, creating affiliate links for those, and recommending them to your clients through your salon. Affiliate marketing is the most effective way to do this.

> "The worst thing you can do is get a second job. The best thing you can do is start a home-based business."
> –Dave Ramsey

Currently, collagen is the hottest beauty trend. Its projected growth is expected to be astronomical within the next several years. We both have linked up with the most potent collagen on the market because our clients were asking us about it, and it made sense for our business.

Lacey studied collagen during the pandemic and educated herself on what the most potent product was and what type of collagen was best for the human body. She found one—Isagenix Collagen Elixir—that's ten times more potent than anything else on the market that actually links up with your own body's collagen peptides after one hundred twenty days. As trusted beauty professionals, it's very important to us to know that anything you recommend is backed by science. The same company actually has an amazing, affordable skincare line, Celletoi, that includes five growth factors, which, to our knowledge, is not included in other types of skincare. At most, a good skincare line will sometimes have three growth factors, and one can expect to pay up to $500 per tube for that. The entire Celletoi line costs less than $250! They have an amazing, patented hair supplement, Hair Revival, that helps regrow hair and revert hair growth cycles back to where they were when we were younger, which totally blew our minds. Did you know that as we age, the anagen (growth) phase cycle shortens, and the catagen and telogen phases lengthen? The patented ingredient is banana flower extract, which is all-natural. The hair growth Lacey has seen on herself and her clients is incredible, and this affiliate company actually, in a roundabout way, introduced Kylie and Lacey to each other!

> "Don't find customers for your product.
> Find products for your customers."
> –Seth Godin

Lacey wasn't really open to affiliate marketing until she was introduced to her first mentor in the space: Gina Redzanic. In fact, the only reason she got on a call with her was because she learned that she was making more than $20,000 each month while working from home and being fully present with her family. She knew that if Gina could do it, then she could do it, too. This was during the pandemic, and her events for the year had been canceled. Her family lost about $100,000 in income that year. They moved back to her hometown in Missouri, and Lacey desperately wanted to stay home with her daughter until she started kindergarten. She took Gina's advice, which was to copy and paste premade posts from Canva on her social media accounts every day for two weeks. At the end of the two weeks, she had made $800, which was enough to cover her next four months of collagen. That is, until the next week, when a medical bill of $756 came, and she needed to use the money for that instead. But the wheels had already been set in motion. Her inbox was blowing up, and she was having fun! She also realized that, in the salon world, her retail bonus checks for the month usually didn't add up to $800, so it was clear to her how powerful this strategy could be in not only the lives of those who used the collagen but also for those who wanted to make extra money from home. The collagen, along with other products she was already paying for, were all now tax-deductible, and she was able to turn something she used every day into extra income.

This made her wonder what other things she was consistently buying that could improve her financial situation. We buy most things online, and a lot of them have an affiliate link we can recommend; Lacey had just never thought to ask about that or had the desire to do so before. Opening herself up to this opportunity led to two paid trips to Mexico within her first two years and even led her to become an author. She knew that making friends with the right people would bring her closer to where she wanted to be. On her first trip, she met at least ten people who were making more than $100,000 per month! Lacey learned about different kinds of investments and ways to make her money work for her. She learned about passive income and how to make money while you sleep. The personal growth she experienced alone was priceless! Lacey met some of her best friends and business partners from different marketing opportunities, and the benefits just keep coming.

Happy Head is another company that provides an affiliate program through which stylists have the opportunity to earn extra income. Kylie wondered how her friend Brenda had a noticeable amount of new hair growing in when she was doing a root retouch service one day. Instantly, the wheels in Kylie's head started turning. How many times have you been asked if you have a solution for thinning hair for men or women? Happy Head has a group of doctors who are board-certified dermatologists and specialize in hair growth. Their products are customized based on one's age, sex, and medical history and are incredibly potent thanks to prescription-grade ingredients such as finasteride, minoxidil, retinoic acid, hydrocortisone, and vitamin D3. This is one of our favorite things to recommend because it offers a large profit margin, and the user's transformation is amazing! When you give someone their dream hair, their change in confidence is instant. People walk taller, hold their shoulders back, and even carry themselves differently! It's what we call "power hair."

Extensions that can be installed in the salon or at home, along with clips, toppers, and wigs, are all potential profit streams. According to Allied Market Research, "The global hair extensions market size was valued at $2.9 billion in 2021 and is projected to reach $6.3 billion by 2031."

Think about that; think about the different things that you wear and love. Maybe your clients always ask you where you bought your clothes or where you got your sunglasses. A few years ago, Lacey fell in love with Zyia Active's clothing line. It was literally the only workout clothing she wanted to wear after discovering that she could see through every other pair of leggings she owned. She became an affiliate to get a discount, and the next thing she knew, a friend asked her if she could host an online party so she could get a discount, too. She hosted several after that and made as much as $1,000 per party! She had fun hosting one online event per month, which didn't require that much time, and made extra money from home. What would you do with an extra $1,000 every month? Jot it down now.

We all post our pictures on social media with Starbucks cups, but we don't make any money from Starbucks for doing so. What if we posted about something that we bought and loved and then made some extra money for it? There are courses that can show you how it's done and expand your network.

And if you're not sure how to make graphics, we've got you! It's not as hard as you might think.

The cost for a salon to acquire new clients used to be almost one hundred dollars, but social media marketing techniques have cut that in half, and becoming an affiliate broadens your scope for exposure even more. Double your network, and you double your net worth!

Six-Figure Stylist Takeaways:

- Identify the elements of your brand.
- What are three different ways you can market yourself in addition to what you're already doing?
- Be mindful of how much time you spend scrolling each day and consider trading some of that for marketing yourself on social media instead.
- Plan a promotion every six to eight weeks for the rest of this year.
- Figure out if your referral program is working.
- What is the one thing you're obsessed with that you aren't monetizing somehow?
- Find the best solution to your salon guests' most prevalent need and become an affiliate with the company that provides it.

"Bonus Resources" to enhance your experience.

- MyGeniusLeads
- Isagenix Collagen, Hair Revival, and Celletoi
- Book a consult for marketing ad campaign help
- Burch Branding consultation

PLEASE SCAN THE QR CODE TO ACCESS:

CHAPTER 4

CREATE AN EXPERIENCE THEY'LL NEVER FORGET

In a world where people have so many choices, you have to give potential clients a reason to choose you. The first twelve seconds after a guest walks into a salon is accompanied by a nervous or uneasy feeling. That's why it's so important for our guests to be greeted in a positive way, whether by the front desk staff or a stylist.

Six-Figure Stylists know that confidence and good posture are everything. The best thing a guest can hear when they enter a salon is their name. For example, when one of your regulars arrives, you might say, "Welcome, Jan! It's so wonderful to see you again!" If you know them well and you're a hugger, you may take a second to hug your guests. If you don't know them well, offer a handshake. In today's world, some people aren't comfortable with that, so read your client. Either way, the last thing we want to do is shout out from the back of the room, "Hey, I'll meet you back at the bowl!"

Lacey recalls going to a new nail salon after moving to Houston. She was nervous, but the place was conveniently located and aesthetically pleasing, so she decided to give it a shot. After all, as beauty professionals, we tend to take our nails very seriously. She stood at the front desk for what felt like several minutes before someone yelled across the salon, "What do you want?" Before she could even answer, she was told to pick a color. She didn't want to just pick a color. She had questions she wanted answered before sitting down. She did get her nails done there, but the appointment only went south from there; it included a ruined spray tan, insults, and a bloody toe. Needless to say, this salon did not become her new nail home, nor did she ever return. The experience there taught her a lot in terms of what not to do.

Kylie had a similar unpleasant experience, except this jaw-dropping, horrifying experience happened within the walls of her own salon. One of the stylists was running behind that day but still managed to meticulously curl her client's hair. A new guest was not told by the stylist or any other associate that they were behind schedule when she checked in at the front desk and then sat down to wait her turn. In a situation like this, communication is crucial. The unattended guest sat and stewed, watching as the other client got her hair curled, while the stylist, rather than tag in the associate helping her, let it happen. The unattended guest went back to the front to ask why, and the team tried to resolve the issue by getting her started with another stylist. The stations are set up like one long island in the middle of the salon, and the guest was seated at the one directly across from her original stylist. They wound up screaming at each other; the client was ticked off about the tardiness and lack of respect for her time, and the stylist proceeded to insult the guest by assuming she wouldn't or couldn't pay her rate for the service she wanted.

So, let's paint a better picture. Six-Figure Stylists have a plan for when they run behind schedule, and it includes taking five seconds to text the guest prior to their appointment time and letting them know about the situation, then thanking them for their patience and understanding. We are never too busy to be respectful, and who knows? Maybe they'll even grab you a coffee during the time they had to spare.

After the greeting comes the consultation, and a Six-Figure Stylist knows how to knock this out of the park! As we approach our chair for the consultation, we like to pull up a cutting stool and sit with the guest. If the chair next to you is open, that could work, too. The last thing you want to do is have the client face the mirror while you touch their hair and talk to them in the mirror. It doesn't always occur to us because we are so comfortable in the salon space, but the guest might view that as impersonal. Ask permission to touch their hair after you sit down and talk with them. Really get to know them while you conduct an analysis of their lifestyle and how that might relate to their haircare routine. Take notes as you go; you can use salon software, a clipboard, or your phone to keep track of all the details. What do they do for a living? What do they like to do with their weekends? Do they garden? Do they swim? Are they in a rock band? Who are they as a person? These are all things that we can use to better evaluate their hair and beauty needs as well as get to know their style. A tone analysis helps us choose the right shades if they're interested in color services; plus, people love knowing whether they are warm- or cool- or even neutral-toned and why you're suggesting the colors that you are. This could be their first time with this, and if you make an impression on them, we bet they'll tell their friends. When we started implementing these practices, sales and referrals went through the roof!

Figure out their facial shape and share with them what it is and why this is important. You might suggest placing their color differently or parting their hair differently based on the shape of their face. Maybe they have a round or square face, and the first thing they do when they sit down is complain about having a "fat face." You can shade the sides to draw the eyes in with a darker color or draw the eyes up with a lighter shade in the front or on the top to elongate their appearance. If they have a longer face, you may want to do the opposite and use a lighter color on the sides. No matter the shape, you can use color to enhance their favorite features and diminish the ones they don't love. While you're at it, identify their high and low side. Maybe switching their part to the opposite side would balance out their look. Maybe they are unaware that everyone has a high and low side. Having a plan and a solution proves your credibility while you build their client's confidence in you.

Have them walk you through their everyday routine. Do they brush their hair prior to getting in the shower? What kind of brush do they use? What's in their shower, and how much of it do they use at a time? How often do they shampoo and condition their hair? What kind of brush do they use on their hair when it's wet? Do they use a blow dryer, and if so, what kind of brush do they use with it? Do they use a nozzle on the blow dryer? Is heat being used on their hair through some other tool or process? If so, what heat protection do they use? Do they use dry shampoo? How do they apply it? Are they using a primer? How are they extending the style? What other products do they have? Maybe what they're using is counterproductive to what they're trying to achieve, but they don't know it because they ordered it on Amazon without any advice from a beauty professional. Maybe they're trying to get volume, but what they're using is way too heavy. Maybe they're using something that's making their hair too oily. Maybe they should use a shampoo with sulfates, or maybe they'd be better off going sulfate-free. Do they have a satin pillowcase? How do they wear their hair while they sleep? These are all questions that we need to ask during the consultation. It may sound like a lot, but it's imperative that we get to the root of their problems before we do anything with their hair.

Perhaps you want to integrate digital consultations to help you find out what they like and what they don't. Ask if there is one thing they would want you to improve or how you can make them love their hair even more. What's their beauty budget? What time can they commit to the service and maintenance at home? How often can they come back? Have them show you a picture of the look they want. Usually, if they are a new guest or if they want a dramatic change, we'll ask them to send in a photo of what their hair looks like now, too.

As you talk, repeat back to the guest what they're sharing to show you're actively listening and to make sure nothing is left to interpretation. Then, you can explain what you will be doing with the rest of their visit, how much time it's going to take, and your rate. The last thing we want is for the guest to experience sticker shock when it's time to pay. Establish a beauty plan and come to an agreement with the client on when they will return next, the details of execution, the time it will all take, and the cost.

A Six-Figure Stylist knows what their hourly rate is. What is your time worth? Make sure you keep that question in mind during the consultation. Hair is hair, but not all hair takes the same amount of time to treat or style.

You'll also want to set the stage for the products you'll recommend during the visit. We've learned that if you want to sell three products, you'll need to use a minimum of six. If you want to sell six of one particular product, you need to have twelve on the shelf. Products should be front-facing, pulled to the front of the shelf, organized, aesthetically pleasing, and packed in close together. These laws of merchandising come from Peter Millard, a designer based in New York who focuses on retail spaces in the beauty industry. His design solutions are strategically tailored to boost retail sales for brands like Redken, Ralph Lauren, Tom Ford, Armani, Essie, L'Oreal, and Chanel.

We also recommend keeping the overall vibration high in the salon. We talked about checking our own personal vibe in earlier chapters, but each salon has its own vibration, too. Music with a good beat and uplifting lyrics vibrates at a higher frequency than something melancholy or angry. Think about what music puts you in a great mood. Smells can affect your buying habits. A study by Washington State University exposed consumers to a simple citrus smell while they shopped. The study revealed that the 100 consumers who shopped with the simple scent in the air spent an average of 20 percent more. (Source: wsu.edu.) We love blood orange essential oil because it is such a happy scent. Remember that happiness, fun, and laughter are all on the same vibrational frequency as money.

The art of professionalism requires finesse. You're not just consulting with a guest; you're creating a guest experience. Lacey was blessed enough to get certified to facilitate L'Oreal's Salon Emotion program. It's a class that empowers beauty professionals to increase profits by knowing how to elevate the guest experience. Through this class, she learned that there are seven touchpoints in the salon:

1. Physical and digital windows attract guests.
2. The reception area should make them feel welcome.

3. Consultations should impress the guest.
4. The treatment lounge or shampoo area should encourage the guests to relax.
5. Services are the big transformation reveal (After the services are performed, the transformation takes place, and the new look is revealed).
6. The retail space empowers the guest to achieve their favorite looks at home.
7. When they check out, the guest needs to feel cared for enough to schedule their next visit.

People want and need an experience to remember. They'll either recall that it was awful or that it was the best salon visit they've ever had. When people leave reviews, it's almost always because of a bad experience; even if they had a fantastic time, they probably won't even think to leave a review unless they're asked to.

While working in Tampa, Lacey once went to a restaurant with some colleagues. The food was pretty good, but their server really went above and beyond to make sure that the experience overall was nothing short of great. When it was time to leave, he handed them his business card (which was a first from a server) and kindly asked that if they enjoyed dinner and the service, to leave him a five-star review on Yelp. Before the Uber arrived, all three of them had downloaded the app and left the server a glowing review. Lacey learned quite a few things from that server. As beauty professionals, we have an advantage because we have our clients' phone numbers. We can set up post-appointment text messages to ask for positive reviews. We could have a QR code on our mirror that would take them straight to where they can leave their feedback, or we could make this part of checking out.

> *"I've learned that people will forget what you said, people will forget what you did, but people will never forget how you made them feel."*
> –Maya Angelou

Think about the best customer service experience you've ever had. Lacey's is the time she stayed at the St. Regis Hotel in New York City. She was greeted by name and immediately felt like royalty in a palace! A butler took her up to her suite and showed her around the suite; they even offered to unpack her bags and iron her clothes. If she wanted, she could request that they turn down the bed and draw her a bath at night, and there was a special phone that would connect her to the butler's personal line. If she decided she wanted champagne and chocolate-covered strawberries at three in the morning, she'd get it. The hotel offered to take her to Grand Central Station in the hotel car, which was a Rolls-Royce. It was raining that day, so they carried an umbrella for her. They even offered to pack her bags for her when it was time to check out! Her stay was a truly memorable experience.

This made her think of ways to enhance the guest experience in the salon—especially on rainy days. What do your guests remember about their experience in your salon? Do you have umbrellas they can borrow if it's raining when they're ready to go and don't want to get their hair wet on the way to their car? Do you send them off in a processing cap? Does anybody give new guests a tour on arrival? Are there signature snacks or a coffee bar? What's the protocol for when a guest is with you all day? Think about what you can offer that would not only surpass their expectations but make the experience so memorable that whether or not they'll be back isn't in question.

Go to a spa, the Four Seasons, or whatever the nicest place is near you and see what they're doing. Try booking a room at the Ritz Carlton for your next special occasion just to observe their customer service policies. Then, brainstorm about how you could do it better. We always want to create and improve on value so we can set ourselves apart from everybody else. This starts with the consultation and guest experience.

Lacey has been friends with a salon guest, Lou Lou, since she started doing her hair fifteen years ago. When Lou Lou was diagnosed with a debilitating disease, and then when she struggled with addiction, Lacey was among the first to know. When Lou Lou lost her dad, they prayed and cried together. Lacey came in on her day off to give her a blowout and help her pick out a dress for her father's funeral because she was too grief-stricken to even think. Lou Lou has confided in her about domestic violence, her finances, affairs, divorce, and all her deepest, darkest secrets. Lacey even invited her to her home on Christmas after her divorce so she wouldn't be alone for the holiday. Once, Lacey even traded her the new shirt she was wearing at the salon when Lou Lou needed something special to wear. Lou Lou keeps a note in her purse with her phone number on it so that, upon her death, her family can call Lacey and have her do her hair. To this day, she tells Lacey that she is the only reason she doesn't need therapy.

Hairdressers hear it all when the cape comes on. A lot of us know every secret of the person in our chair. We've learned that people do not want sympathy; they need empathy. They want someone to listen, not give them advice. They need to be heard without the listener voicing their opinions.

> *"Empathy fuels connection & sympathy drives disconnection.*
> *Empathy is feeling with people."*
> –Brené Brown

Nursing scholar Teresa Wiseman studied different professions where empathy was most relevant and came up with four qualities of empathy:

1. The ability to understand the perspective of another person or recognize their perspective as their truth.
2. Resisting the urge to pass judgment.
3. Recognizing emotion in other people.
4. Communication.

Six-Figure Stylists can read the room and control the conversation as needed. Sometimes, a guest's low vibe is palpable. Our goal should always be to try and make them feel better by the time they're ready to go. They might complain about their husband, an ex-boyfriend, or their mother-in-law. They don't need your advice, so you can let it go in one ear and out the other. We hear a lot, and we cannot possibly hold all that in on top of anything we've got going on in our own lives. So, find where you can connect with that person, and then listen. If you can't help but say something, simply tell them you're glad they felt comfortable enough with you to share and that you're there for them. You're not an expert, though you may think you are.

Don't host complaining sessions with your client about what's going on in your life. They love you, but they don't care. They didn't come to hear about your problems; they came for your services. When we control the conversation, we teach them more about self-care. Maybe they've unloaded on you for a while, and you've just listened patiently, but you can't take it anymore. That's okay—we've all been there! A good transition might sound something like, "I don't mean to interrupt you, but this is the part you'll need to be able to recreate when you get home." Or "I'm going to need you to apply the product like this. What side is easiest for you to style?" Then, you can get them involved in learning how to mimic the look for themselves, which is why they came to you in the first place. Have them work on the side they find challenging so you can watch and instruct them on how to hold the blow dryer or brush. That way, you can keep the vibe upbeat but also deliver on the service they're paying you for.

We used to work with a stylist who was a habitual complainer and had a consistently low vibe. Every conversation was the same, and it was all about her. We rarely heard her clients talk while they were in her chair. In fact, she eventually lost most of her clients. But in the meantime, they got to hear all about how her boyfriend treated her badly and how she was on government assistance. There's nothing wrong with needing or accepting help, but a salon guest doesn't need to know about it. She never had any money but didn't want to make too much because that would interfere with her eligibility for assistance. This kind of shop talk was not only unprofessional, but it was detrimental to her career. She ended up leaving the salon because she wasn't busy enough. Where focus goes, energy flows!

We all need to be mindful of this, not just in the hair world. Because of the close relationships we share with our guests, it's easy to forget that we are professionals. The friendship must stay one-sided when you're behind the chair. When someone shares a story, it's too easy to share one in return that then makes it about you instead of them. They share with you because you are a safe place. You may be the only one they can tell certain things to. They never share because they actually want to hear about you and your experiences.

We find it helpful to clear the energy between guests whenever possible. Go outside for a change of scenery. Sometimes, a mental break is necessary because energy is contagious. It's no wonder, at the end of the day, most stylists find themselves sitting silently in their car for a few minutes. It's important to recharge yourself after a full day of hyperstimulation. A bustling salon full of people talking over blow dryers is a lot to take in, so take time for yourself. Maybe consider adding an extra thirty minutes at the end of your workday for solitude or meditation, especially if you have a family at home waiting for you. When we don't refill our cups, we have nothing left to give to those who need anything—physically or emotionally—from us.

Lacey once did a challenge at a salon that she worked in. The idea was to go twenty-one whole days without complaining. If you have a problem, go directly to the source with a solution. She had a bracelet, and each time she complained, even in her mind, she had to switch it to the other wrist. Going three weeks without complaining is hard! This made her hyper-aware of herself and those around her, and it really helped her identify who didn't want to be around.

She found tools she could use to avoid getting drawn into complaining and its low vibe. After that first challenging week, she felt so much happier.

This continued, and it was truly life-changing! Even her husband noticed the difference and asked about it. Her numbers at work also increased; at the time, she didn't know about the law of vibration, but now she realizes that she was starting to operate on a higher frequency. Everything we do, think, or say has a vibration. It's all energy, and it shows in the money we make. At the end of this chapter, we'll have a resource on this for you.

Six-Figure Stylists dress the part because even the way we dress has a vibration. If you want successful days at the salon, you need to dress for it. You can't show up in sweatpants and a sports bra, makeup-free, and with your hair in a messy bun, then expect to make bank. You have to dress for the career you want, not necessarily for the one you have. We were once told that we should look like we're in a magazine every day because we're in the beauty industry. Think about what you'd wear to style hair at NYFW when you dress for work. The better you look, the better you feel. When we look better, we carry ourselves with more confidence. Get in those circles. Ask for those referrals. It's all about achieving a higher vibration and maintaining that momentum.

A few years ago, Kylie experimented with her look. One day, she didn't dress up as much as she usually did, and her hair didn't look its best. On another day, she dressed up, and her hair and makeup were on point. That day, she made way more money, raked in more tips, and sold more retail items. The better you feel about yourself—because of the way you dress and because of your physical health—equates to a higher vibration, and a higher vibration equals more money.

When Lacey became a salon owner at the age of twenty-five, she decided she needed to raise the bar regarding her appearance. While she always did her hair and makeup before work, she wanted to be taken more seriously in the business world. It's hard enough to do that when you're young and don't look the part. Her prices were doubling, and she was moving about fifteen miles away, so she expected to lose quite a few clients. She knew that she had to set a precedent for how she wanted everyone else to dress. Lacey did lose a lot of salon guests. However, this made room for others. That year, she went from seeing about a hundred salon guests each month to seeing over two hundred twenty-five in the same span! Her referrals were through the roof, retail sales were booming, and she was more confident. All of her guests noticed the upgrade in her appearance; in fact, she still has a few laughs with some of them about the Crocs that used to make the occasional appearance behind the chair in her early career.

But while her wardrobe improved, being a new salon owner combined with infertility stress and hormone therapy was taking a toll on her physical appearance. She wasn't able to work out often due to fertility treatments and medication, and she didn't always make her physical health a priority. Eating out often, too much Starbucks, a lack of sleep, and the stress of losing her mom didn't help. Her weight reached an all-time high, and her self-esteem took a hit. She actually cried in a dressing room when she tried on something in the biggest size the store carried, but it didn't fit. She cried when her brother-in-law assumed she was pregnant (no more leggings and empire waists for her after that). After selling her half of the salon to take care of her mom in her final stages, Lacey decided she had better start taking better care of herself. She realized that life is too short for regrets and to not have everything the way she wanted it. She decided to take charge of her physical appearance and started running again; she even signed up for a half marathon to keep herself accountable. This did wonders for her mental health because running releases endorphins and allows us time to think, process, and visualize.

It was while she was running along ice and snow that she decided her next step would be to become a certified Redken Artist. In the meantime, she'd visualize how she would look and feel being on stage and working with people that she'd only dreamed of working with—like Sam Villa—although her ex-husband warned her not to dream too big because "not everybody can do that." Challenge accepted! She also helped start a weight loss challenge at the salon where she worked. She won after dropping thirty pounds in three months! She ran her first half marathon (without even stopping) and auditioned to become a certified Redken Artist. She wouldn't have had the confidence to do any of this if her outward appearance had remained the same. She was finally her confident self again, and it was time her wardrobe reflected it. To be a Redken Artist, one must be on trend and dress to impress! Our motto is that it's always better to be the best-dressed person in the room. And while body positivity is important, let's not confuse it with accepting and praising an unhealthy body that we aren't confident or comfortable in.

Six-Figure Stylists specialize for greater success. As a national educator and platform artist, Lacey was told that she couldn't be a jack-of-all-trades because that would make her the master of none. So, she became a color expert, and being a Redken Certified Haircolorist is like having a PhD in color techniques. It also landed her a spot on the Redken salon finder site, so when someone goes looking for a certified colorist in their zip code, her name pops up. In order to get booked as an educator for classes and shows, she had to be all in. If she took a class, it had to be a class on color. Each time she took a class at the Redken Exchange in New York or somewhere else, she would receive a new certification and a press release. It also helped her create loads of content for her social media accounts. These classes also put her in front of some incredibly talented artists. She gained so much wisdom from her mentors; having people you can reach out to with questions is priceless. She also got contracts with some of the best in the industry: Sam Villa, Kris Sorbie, Justin Isaac, Randy Topham, Julie Lahr, Ty Isobe, Jayson Morgan, Ryan Morgan, Lori Zabel, Jesse Linares, and Scott Sueper. All of this work helped shape her skillset as an educator and hairstylist, her reputation, and her brand, ultimately earning her more money.

Several years ago, Lacey moved from Missouri to Texas. She didn't know anyone except the owner of the salon because she was also a certified Redken Artist. A client came in and asked for corrective color. The front desk attendant placed her with Lacey because she knew that she was the color expert. She had Level 2 hair and four-inch regrowth with a red/violet box dye on it; she wanted to be Level 10 platinum. She was a college student who had obviously done her homework. She told Lacey she wanted all the treatments in between and post-color. She informed her that she had been saving for two years to do this, had $2,000 to spend, and did not want to risk the integrity of her hair. Lacey spent about four to five hours each day for two days on her, and she came back every four weeks, becoming one of her best clients. Because Lacey posted online about this corrective color job, she became known as the corrective color and blonding expert in town. Everybody who needed corrective color or was going from a dark hair color to platinum ended up in her chair, all because she decided to become an expert in something and used her social media wisely. The first place someone looks when they consider hiring someone is their social media accounts. Lacey's brand and experience speak for themselves.

Most guests say that the shampoo is their favorite part of a visit to the salon. In other words, if you give them a good shampoo, even if you then give them a bad haircut, they're probably going to come back to see you. Make your shampoo area a treatment lounge. We recommend having a signature shampoo system that all of your stylists know and then spreading the word that your salon is known for giving the best shampoo in town. Take a class or go somewhere else and have your hair shampooed, including a scalp massage with a conditioning treatment, so you can see how others do it. We release endorphins from the top of our heads, which makes people feel good. People who feel good are happier and spend more money. So, don't skimp out on the shampoo or the massage. In fact, offer add-on services related to the shampoo, like conditioning treatments. If your conditioning treatment stays on for five minutes, give them a five-minute scalp massage while it sets in. You could even look into getting a lesson from a massage therapist.

If you don't get your hair done at your own salon, maybe you need to give that a try so you can evaluate the customer experience firsthand. On top of conditioning treatments, we provide eye treatments, hand and arm massages, paraffin treatments, and several types of facial waxing. You have the potential to earn extra income at the shampoo bowl without wasting time, and that can really add up.

Let's say you offer a conditioning treatment that takes five minutes. You don't need to add extra time to somebody's appointment to add that on, and you talked to them about it during the consultation. You've done their color treatment, so you know that their pH level needs to be rebalanced. It might be more or a little less, depending on where you are, but let's just say it costs $25 for this example. If you see five guests in a day and two people take you up on it, that's fifty bucks per day. If you work five days a week, that's an extra $250 each week. Now, let's assume you take two weeks of vacation, so you work fifty weeks in a year. That translates to an extra $12,500 in services. Divide that in half, and that means you get an extra $6,250 in a year without having to add extra time.

Daily Earnings Calculation:
Daily Earnings $= 2 \times \$25 = \$50$

Weekly Earnings Calculation:
Weekly Earnings $= \$50 \times 5 = \$250$

Annual Earnings Calculation:
Annual Earnings $= \$250 \times 50 = \$12,500$

Personal Annual Gain Calculation:
Personal Annual Gain $= \$12,500 \div 2 = \$6,250$

Pause right now and consider what you would do with an extra $6,250 this year without adding time to your books. Make a note of that right now to set the intention of giving yourself a raise. You're worth it, and your salon guests will love getting pampered.

Presentation is everything to beauty consultants, and Six-Figure Stylists are also beauty consultants. They are professional. They do everything with purpose. They attend educational events regularly and dress to impress. They also use positive affirmations to keep themselves focused on their goals. Even if you don't believe them all now, start speaking them into existence anyway. If you're not sure where to start, try these.

- I am a Six-Figure Stylist.
- I am a money magnet.
- I am successful.
- I am talented.
- I am smart.
- I am beautiful.
- I am an insanely awesome hairstylist.
- I am fearfully and wonderfully made.
- I am blessed with more than enough clients.
- I am worthy.
- I am full of favor.
- I attract so much abundance in all areas of my life.
- I attract clients who love my work and can easily afford my prices.
- It feels so good to work less and make much more.

Some stylists are stuck in job mode. They complain about having to go to a class that their boss has paid for; they usually don't take the initiative to go to a class on their own, let alone pay for it themselves. They don't dress for success or wear makeup when they arrive—not always on time. They pass off walk-ins to someone else in favor of scrolling on their phone. They never want to stay late, and they don't recommend products. They have a low vibe, so it's no wonder they don't make much money.

Six-Figure Stylists educate their salon guests. Starting statements with "my professional recommendation is" makes you sound like a true beauty consultant, not "just a hairstylist." You care about more than hair, and you're more experienced. As such, your language affects how clients speak to and about you. You teach them how to do what they're asking you to do so they learn to recreate their look at home. You make sure to have every single thing they'll need either physically in your salon or available to check out by a link on your phone. And instead of them going to TikTok or YouTube to learn new ways to style their hair, try setting up a tripod with their phone so they have their own tutorial on how to style their hair a certain way. Take charge, and before you take the client's cape off, say, "My professional recommendation is that you go home with X, Y, and Z today." Remember that if we recommend six products, they're probably going home with at least three of them. They may say, "I can only get three of those today." In that case, respond with, "I'll make a note of what you're going to need next time."

Adopt an interactive, innovative approach at the salon. Authenticity sells. You can have a mannequin handy or even in the retail area for salon guests to try products out. You could teach a mom a new braid for their daughter while their color is processing if you don't have another guest to attend to. Maybe you could have elastics in a bowl next to a product they can use to coat the elastic and prevent breakage, as well as help it slip out of their updos more easily. You could have an iron and a heat protector next to the mannequin so they can try out a new curl or tool. You could have grips in a bowl of mattifying powder to inspire questions and to show off a new way to use a product, creating value while you're at it.

Six-Figure Stylist Takeaways:

- Identify areas you can elevate in your career.
- What changes can you make to the retail area to add more value for your salon guests?
- Make positive affirmations part of your daily routine.
- Dress for success.
- Make the most of your consultations.
- Establish your hourly rate.
- What are you going to do with the raise you are giving yourself this year thanks to what you'll earn from add-on services?

"Bonus Resources" to enhance your experience.
- Master your consultations
- Retail scripts and tips

PLEASE SCAN THE QR CODE TO ACCESS:

Resources:

- *A Complaint Free World: How to Stop Complaining and Start Enjoying the Life You Always Wanted* by Will Bowen
- Brené Brown on Empathy vs Sympathy
- L'Oreal's Salon Emotion program
- *Reinventing Space the Clear Logic to Successful Salon Design and Retail Merchandising* by Peter Millard

CHAPTER 5

WORK SMARTER, NOT HARDER

You've all probably heard the phrase, "Work smarter, not harder." But what does this mean?

What makes your salon or even your suite unique? What systems do you have in place to create a pleasant, sensible workflow the moment guests walk through the door? Do you have check-in and check-out processes? Do they look the same for every guest? Do you utilize an assistant or associates? Do you double-book? We all have systems in place, whether we realize it or not. You might be surprised to learn that a whopping 47% of our day is based on ritual. (Source: web.colby.edu.) Our brains go on autopilot to help us out. So, let's streamline our days with purpose. Without systems, we are unorganized, and trust us, salon guests can tell. Plus, effective systems are a crucial part of working smarter, not harder.

Let's start with the front desk. The front desk is not just a station for the receptionist. Imagine walking into any retail store to find the employees sitting, scrolling on their phones, and unwilling to help or even stand up. Whoever mans the front desk has probably one of the most significant roles in the entire salon; they are the equivalent of the quarterback on a football team. If things don't run smoothly at the front of the house, there will be chaos everywhere else. The front desk also includes the whole retail area. Receptionists have to be educated on the products and should be able to recognize any additional opportunities to book add-on services. They also help the team close sales, book future appointments, and confirm existing ones. Adding on services can often be done during these confirmation calls.

A great resource on offering opportunities like these is the book *The Magic in Asking High Vibrational Questions* by Bill Mayer. This book teaches us how to ask questions in such a manner that we often get the answers we want. It truly is one of the best secrets in our toolbox! The front desk staff should make all new guests feel welcome by giving them a salon tour, offering a beverage and time to browse any current specials, and informing them of the loyalty program if you have one. We recommend finding someone friendly and energetic, who can multitask, perform well under pressure, and who has some sales experience. This can be challenging, as Kylie can attest. She's found that some candidates possess fantastic computer skills but have no personality. Or, they are super friendly and personable, but can't get a handle on the salon systems and booking procedure.

Take the time to find the right person for the front of the house. The front desk is responsible for the client's first impression of the whole salon, and it's a lasting one. A variety of studies have been done regarding how quickly we make first impressions. Some say it takes up to fifteen seconds, the average being seven seconds. However, two psychologists from Princeton concluded that it takes a tenth of a second to form a first impression. Think about experiences you've had with first impressions, then decide what you want your salon to say about you.

In our salon company, we have four-step check-in and check-out processes. You can laminate these systems and place them on the front desk for easy reference. Feel free to borrow ours and customize them to suit your needs.

Check In:

1. "Welcome to [*name of salon*], [*Client name if you know it*]. It's great to see you again. I'll let [*stylist's name*] know you're here. I know she is looking forward to her visit with you today, and we hope you enjoy your time with us."
2. After they are checked in, make sure the client is aware of retail promotions. "Just so you know, we have a buy more/save more promotion going on. Let your stylist know if you have any questions as to which product is right for you."
3. Next, offer them add-on services if there is room on the schedule. "It looks like [*stylist name*] has time in her schedule to do a deep conditioning or a gloss service today. Do you have time for that? And which of those would you like?"
4. Let them browse and get them a beverage if they'd like one. For new clients or walk-ins, point out the restrooms and offer a tour of the salon. Do not tell them to sit. The idea is to keep them engaged in the retail area when they aren't with their stylist. "Feel free to shop around. [*Stylist name*] will be with you shortly."

Check Out:

1. Asking clients about their experience is extremely important. This allows the client to tell you what they liked or disliked so the salon can salvage the situation if all did not go well. Genuine guest feedback on your business is one of the best tools for improvement.
2. Offer recommendations as to which products the client will want to take home with them. "Your stylist recommended these three products for you to use to recreate your look. Would you like to go ahead and purchase them before you go?" The rule of thumb is that if you bring up three, they'll at least take one, which is good because part of the service is making sure they can maintain the style themselves at home.

3. Booking their next appointment at this point makes it more likely they'll get in on their preferred day and time rather than waiting until they're desperate. It's also an insurance policy on your future income. "[*Stylist name*] would like to see you back in six weeks. Would the same time work for you on [*day of the week, month, day*]?"
4. "Thank you so much, [*client name*], for your visit today. We look forward to seeing you next time. If you loved your experience with us today, please leave a review."

Hopefully, that will help you become more comfortable with checking clients in and out. This will become second nature if you consistently offer each element you include in your own lists.

Six-Figure Stylists double-book to maximize their time. Benjamin Franklin's advice to a young tradesman was, "Remember that time is money." Our two most valuable resources are time and money. We certainly don't need to mindlessly scroll through our social media feeds while one client's color is processing, especially when we could be doing a quick haircut, another application, or a number of various other services. Some salons offer an associate training program that pairs new stylists with one of the busier master stylists in the salon. This gives the master stylist an extra set of hands so they can help two or three guests at a time. To maximize your time, you either need to charge more and perform more services per guest or double-book guests. If you have an associate training program in place, then you should be able to do a combination of both while providing top-notch services.

An associate training program makes it easier for a stylist to transition from a school environment to a professional salon environment. When new stylists graduate from school, they often need to be taught how to do more than just pass the state board. When you get out in the real world, you gain most of your experience. An assistant is used, and an associate is taught. Any additional information these new stylists can soak up from a veteran stylist puts them light-years ahead, but only if they stay engaged and pay attention.

Kylie's experience in working with associates is that it not only maximizes time but also helps preserve her body, all while the new associates receive hands-on experience in client interaction in a safe space. For stylists like her, who have blow-dried and shampooed for more than twenty years, an associate program is great. Our job is a physical one, and it can take a toll on the body. However, you have to teach the associates how you want processes like shampooing and styling done before they can start taking things off your plate. For example, anybody can rough dry their hair and throw together some kind of style. An associate should be taught to deliver a beautiful blowout while teaching the guest what products to use as well as why and how to recreate the finished look at home. Let the associates get involved in processes like helping to formulate color and apply color.

If Kylie is working six hours to twelve hours behind the chair, she's completely present with the person in her chair. The way she looks at it is that the guest has limited time to spend with her, so that's where her focus should be. Kylie's time is also as maximized as she can get it. If she has a break scheduled, it's because she knew that she would need it. Every single minute is intentional; it has to be in order for her to stay on task and organized. When we work with intention, efficiency comes naturally. If Kylie is glazing somebody and needs help blow drying, her associates know exactly what to do. She says, "We've been utilizing an associate program for well over ten years now, and it's like a well-oiled, beauty-making machine."

Sometimes, the conversations we have with guests can get interesting, and sometimes, we need to steer them back to a more professional topic. Having a code word or a signal can discreetly let the team know that it's time to get back on task. Some salons use different things; Kylie has even used a hot pink comb to reel the conversation back into safer waters. We have a similar system for if somebody needs help. Teamwork makes the dream work, and in our salon, teamwork makes all the difference in what kind of day we're all going to have. At some point, everyone falls behind, but if we can help and support one another, then the crisis can be averted. Most importantly, as owners and mentors, we would never ask someone to do something we aren't willing to do ourselves. Lead by example and have a strategy in place for all aspects of the salon's operation.

Book a little extra time for new guests since you don't always know how long you will need with them, and also know your application times. If you double-book, you always need to know where you are in the schedule for the day. Kylie frequently asks her associates to report on where everyone is on the schedule. Why? Because we double- or even triple-book sometimes, and time is valuable, it's not to be wasted or taken lightly. When a guest arrives, and you are running behind, it is crucial to acknowledge them as quickly as possible. Think about an experience in which you felt your time wasn't valued and how you felt as a result. Think of something you could offer a guest to soften the blow a little if you're behind schedule and they have to wait. If we know we are running more than fifteen minutes behind, a simple text letting the guest know about the situation is much appreciated. We typically need extra time for consultations with new guests, and if we are not working with an assistant or an associate, then we will likely not be able to double-book on that person. The other option is to offer a virtual consultation to avoid wasting time. Know who you have coming in, but maximize your time to curb burnout.

Just like other types of professionals, many hairstylists run the risk of burning out after so many years. It's usually because they haven't maximized their time. Consider what two hours of your time is worth, and write it down right now. In two hours, most stylists can finish at least $200 in services. Let's look at the money. If you work five days a week and sit around for two hours on each of those days, that's $1,000 you've lost each week. If you take two weeks of vacation that year, that's $50,000 lost or approximately $25,000 you could be making annually.

Hourly Services Calculation:
Services in Two Hours = $200

Weekly Lost Earnings Calculation:
Weekly Lost Earnings = $200 × 5 = $1,000

Annual Lost Earnings Calculation:
Annual Lost Earnings = $1,000 × 50 = $50,000 (assuming 50 work weeks per year)

Potential Annual Gain Calculation:
Potential Annual Gain = $50,000 ÷ 2 = $25,000

Think about what you could do with an extra $25,000 per year, especially considering it would compound over time. We are talking millions if you're smart about it. Write it down now.

Learn to live on less, or at least stick to the same amount of money you spend now, even when you see your profits increase. You don't need to drive a Mercedes or buy a bigger home to impress everyone else. When we give ourselves a raise, what we do with it matters. Most feel the need to improve their status with objects, but people don't get rich like that. People who invest their money get more money, and at some point in your career, this is more important than the superficial stuff.

> *"When are we going to stop buying things to impress people that don't matter?"*
> –Dave Ramsey

If a Six-Figure Stylist is reading a book, it's for personal or professional development. If they're on their phone, it's to post on social media, plan content, or learn something new. If they have downtime at the salon, it's been planned for ahead of time. You can avoid burning out by creating the salon schedule that you want based on your life and your family's needs. Don't miss every single soccer game, wedding, or family dinner if you don't absolutely have to. Twenty years ago, new beauty professionals often worked every night and every Saturday. And sometimes, it takes those long hours to build your schedule and your client list. Evenings and weekends are when most working people are available. There is a time and place for the grind; just don't get stuck in it for too long.

At the start of Lacey's career, she waited tables and bartended to pay the bills while working at least forty hours each week in the salon, including every Saturday. She also had a DJ business that kept her booked most Saturday and sometimes Friday nights. She knew that most people needed salon appointments to take place in the evening or on Saturdays, so that's how she booked hers. Unless she was already scheduled to work for another job, almost no appointment time was off-limits. Thank goodness she didn't have children then! At her first salon, the Saturday hours were nine in the morning to two in the afternoon. When she filled up her schedule, she'd book even earlier and come in at four-thirty in the morning if needed. She would book wedding hair, then DJ the reception after work. She learned to cross-promote her businesses. Was it hard work? Yes. Did it pay off? It only took her three and a half years in the industry to open her own successful salon and spa, so yes!

Opening the salon took up even more of her time, but she no longer needed the waitressing job or the DJ business to make ends meet. She went all in on her salon and had a hard time turning her brain off when she wasn't there because a business is always running. There's always more to do, and new ways to make it better. She was willing to stay late when no one else could because you don't turn away business when you start out—especially when you have a shiny new salon to pay for. The price of success isn't cheap, and it doesn't come without sacrifices. Lacey was raised on a farm with a sick mom, so at this stage of her life, work was all she knew. It was impressed upon her as a small child that you play when the work is done. But the work was never done, so she just kept at it. And while her work brought her joy, she stopped doing other things that made her happy and even stopped taking care of herself for a while. She wasn't equipped yet with the tools and life lessons that would eventually remind her to schedule time off and to say no sometimes. When we only say yes to everyone else, we're really saying no or taking time away from ourselves. Her health and her confidence took major hits. She lost time with her family and loved ones that she will never get back. If she could go back, she would make a better schedule and stick to it, plan vacations—not just hair-related educational events—and rearrange her schedule when something important came up. She may have taken a week off instead of working through miscarrying twins after her first round of IVF. But then again, she also says she wouldn't change a thing because that was the price she was willing to pay for success. She had to give it her all, and no one else would have done it for her. That's how dreams are made, and she learned from an early age how short life could be. We only have one shot—make it count.

Kylie also has experience trading time for money. In the beginning, she had three jobs: waiting tables, bartending, and doing hair. She did it all until it was no longer necessary. Once she had built up her clientele, she knew she could give up the other two jobs and focus on being a beauty professional. She liked having money and what she could do with it, but pursuing it meant sacrificing time with family and friends, putting leisure activities on the back burner, and missing big events. Who goes back to work four days after having a baby? It sounds insane, but hindsight is twenty-twenty, and you can't beat yourself up over decisions you've already made. You just move on.

Being a hairstylist is what you make of it. But you should also make time for the things that are important to you outside of the salon. Choose a place where you can work, but have a Saturday off once in a while, and make time to do things that refill your cup.

Personal developments often play a big role in raising your prices. When a client loses their job, or the kids go to college, or any number of things happen, we might feel bad about raising prices. But you can't take money out of your own pocket to save someone else's. When you pay more for color or other products, you have to charge your clients more. When the price of oil goes up, gas prices increase, and the consumer takes on that cost. We're often so emotionally connected to our regulars that we sometimes feel guilty for making a genuine profit off them and forget that we are here to make money in order to support our own families and live better lives. Ask your sales reps to give you as much of a heads-up as they can when product prices are due to increase. This happens at least twice a year, but recently, it's been more like four or more times per year. But this way, you can alert your clients to the changes in your rates based on these industry adjustments before you have to implement them in the salon.

While she traveled across the country to educate stylists, Lacey discovered that an alarming number of beauty professionals had not raised their prices in years. They were losing money instead of raising prices just to break even. Who goes to work somewhere and expects or chooses to make less over time and with more experience? It speaks volumes about how much they valued themselves and what they were taught (or not taught) about the business. Lacey would ask these stylists, "Who is more important: your family or your client?" If you're too scared to tell someone that the price for the service they usually get went up a few bucks once or twice a year, then you've got big problems. If you'd rather take away food from your own table or money from your own retirement, vacation, or kids' college funds, then you have to change your mindset. If this is you, please reach out and let us help you. This is one of the reasons we are so passionate about what we do.

> *"If you want to get something you've never had, you must do something you've never done."*
> – Thomas Jefferson

If it doesn't make you happy, that is going to affect your work. For example, Kylie doesn't do vivids, not because there isn't money in it, but because she doesn't enjoy that type of service. She would rather refer those clients to someone who loves doing it. Post about the things that you enjoy, that bring you joy, and that you're best at in order to attract the right type of guest. Kylie once had a queen bee for a regular client: Robyn. Her personality was larger than life, and she loved the finer things. It's very important to find a queen bee (or a few of them) who trusts your work and likes you as a person because they tell all their friends how wonderful you are. Just don't ask for referrals until you have delivered an amazing look and salon experience to build rapport. If you love doing kids' haircuts, then by all means, post about kids' haircuts. But, if you don't want to be stacked up with kids' haircuts and stab yourself five times in one day because they're squirming around too much for you to work, then don't advertise that you'll do them. There's not a lot of money in specializing in kids' haircuts, and it doesn't bring most stylists a lot of joy. It takes a special person to want to work with kids all day, and our hats go off to them. But remember to work smarter, not harder.

A Six-Figure Stylist knows when to fire a client. This one can get tricky, but if they drain your energy and you truly dread seeing them, they have to go. Now, we talked earlier about the lifetime value of clients, but if you see somebody on your books for Wednesday, and it's only Monday, and you're dreading their appointment, then whatever you were going to make from serving that person might not be worth it. At the same time, if your energy changes just because you know this person is coming in and you're dreading it, you're kind of manifesting a bad appointment. This is where a positive mindset comes in; you're stronger than you think you are. Remember that where our focus goes, energy flows.

We take on a lot of energy throughout the day. We hear it all, though we're not trained in psychology or to give advice. Kylie once had a client mention she was thinking about suicide. This certainly wasn't in her wheelhouse, but while the client was processing, she wrote down a few places and phone numbers for her that specialized in this matter and then gave it to her before she left the salon. She made weekly follow-up calls to this client. It's hard when somebody lays something really heavy like that on your shoulders.

Similarly, when we know that a person doesn't make us feel good or that they are never satisfied, no matter how great the quality of our work is, it's time to have a conversation. Kylie had a client like this; let's call her "Pam." Pam was something of a local celebrity and "high maintenance." Pam wanted to always come in on Sundays (when it was closed to everyone else) because she didn't want anyone to see her getting her hair done. Kylie would accommodate her time and time again, even though she wasn't supposed to work on Sundays. One day, Kylie's daughter was sick with strep throat. She called Pam and told her that she'd have to reschedule her appointment because the baby was sick. Pam didn't care and was extremely irritated with her. Kylie explained that she couldn't help the situation—kids get sick—and that their arrangement was no longer going to work. Kylie couldn't believe that after years of catering to this woman, she couldn't be flexible for a sick baby. She also let her know that the way she was acting was unacceptable. It was the last straw, and in that moment, Kylie realized that sometimes we love our clients way more than they love us.

Lacey also once had a similar guest; let's call her "Maria." She was never satisfied, even though Lacey delivered exactly what she asked for. She knew in her heart of hearts that she did everything right, but Maria would always come back in and want her hair redone for free because of one made-up reason or another. She never said anything right away; she would wait until it was almost time to get it done again, sometimes two or three weeks after her appointment. Maria was also habitually late or simply didn't show up for appointments if she didn't call with a last-minute cancellation. This kind of client costs us money and energy, but we also genuinely want our clients to love their hair. Maria is the reason why Lacey implemented a new policy that states that if a client isn't happy with their look, they should let her know within a week of getting it done so she can make it right. She encourages open communication and is not offended if someone has a valid reason for wanting something redone. She is more than happy to make it right because she would much rather guests love their hair than complain about it to everyone they know. However, if a guest decides that they want red hair, and she gives them the red hair they asked for, they're responsible for paying to have it fixed if they freak out and want to revert back to their original color.

We are not responsible if someone dislikes what they asked us to do or if we deliver a look that a guest asked for, but she goes home and her husband or boyfriend doesn't like it. So, Lacey had a private conversation with Maria and didn't allow her to book her next appointment. She said, "You know, I have to be honest. I don't feel like this relationship is working out. I feel like you may be better suited with somebody else because I haven't been able to deliver exactly what you want." This can be done in a kind and professional manner; it does not have to be an awkward scene or a string of ongoing texts.

There's something to be said for keeping a blacklist. If you feel like someone really shouldn't keep coming to the salon, you should add them to it. Sometimes you can reach a compromise, like if the issue arises because they don't want to pay your prices; if you have other stylists at a lower price point, recommend that the client switches to one of them in order to stay within their budget. But there may be a time when you have to block a person from being able to be booked at all. Maybe it's someone who has made you feel uncomfortable or has said or done inappropriate things while in the salon. Just because they were a guest does not mean they have to continue to be. You have a relationship with every person that sits down in your chair. So, if they're better suited to work with somebody else, that's fine. If someone doesn't respect your time and they're a no-show, then you have to do the math and decide whether or not you're willing to fire them, and how that will benefit or harm you.

One time, a guest yelled at Lacey. Lacey had been doing this lady's hair for years and was shocked. They'd had a salon meeting that morning, and the meeting went late. Then, Lacey had to go to the bathroom and prepare before she started the client's two-hour service. She greeted her and apologized for the delay, but before she could explain and begin the consultation, the salon guest began to yell at her. Lacey had come in early for this guest before, but on that particular day, she couldn't get started with her before hours due to the meeting. This person was also habitually late, canceled at the last minute, or didn't show up at all. She'd come in late with Starbucks or McDonalds in hand, or her breath would smell like onions, so it was obvious she'd just eaten in the car. So, Lacey took three deep breaths and waited for her opening to calmly say, "I've never yelled at you for being late. How many times have you been late to your hair appointments?" The client looked at her like a deer caught in headlights, so Lacey continued. "I will not be disrespected this way. You are no longer my client."

It was sad, almost like a breakup after working with her for six years. Lacey was hurt, but she knew that she had to stand up for herself because what you permit, you promote. Sometimes, you need to implement a policy for no-shows and people who are always late. You could try a three-strike policy or make it so that if someone doesn't show up to their appointment or at least call ahead, they have to pay half the cost anyway. Sometimes, you need to be vulnerable and honest with your salon guests. You can tell someone that when they choose not to come to their appointment or just forget, you don't make money. Lacey would ask, "If you go to work, do you make the same amount of money the whole time you're there? Because when I don't have a guest in my chair, I'm not making money, and you haven't given me an opportunity to fill your spot." You have to be straight with them and tell them that you simply can't afford to do business like that because this is how you pay your bills and put food on the table.

The truth is, Lacey should've fired that guest long before she ever yelled at her. The yelling simply pushed her over the line. We all understand that sometimes things happen, and we all run late, but there needs to be a certain level of mutual respect involved. One-sided relationships never work out, and sometimes, some people have to figure out boundaries the hard way. Weigh the pros and cons when you consider parting ways with a client, and put some policies in place that establish your boundaries. These can be detailed in writing or talked about during a consultation. If you've been seeing a guest for a long time but are just now implementing these policies, let them know what they are and help them understand why they're necessary now. Our hope in sharing these personal stories is that you can learn from our mistakes and find a better way to navigate these challenges.

Let's switch gears and talk about smart scheduling! We've already discussed double-booking and utilizing our associates, but if we have time in our day and can work somebody else in, we are not above calling or texting someone to see if they would be willing to shift their appointment. We don't want to get in the habit of frequently asking everybody to come in earlier so we can leave earlier, but utilizing any free time in your books is smart. Your front desk employees should be trained to do this automatically, as well as streamline your operations for efficiency's sake. They can make product sales for you over the phone while confirming appointments. Or, if you confirm your own appointments, you can make those offers before clients come in so the sales are not always last-minute. To be a Six-Figure Stylist, you also have to pre-book appointments before clients leave. At the end of this chapter, we will have scripts you can use to reference for this practice.

As new stylists, we would ask all of our clients when they needed to come in next. It took us a few years to learn what a mistake that was. For example, when Lacey was still a fairly new salon owner, she was getting a lot of new clients, but the retention rate was low and the pre-book percentage wasn't great. If the latter is only about 50%, your retention is probably the same. You have to gain momentum quickly when you have a new salon and figure out how to maintain it. It does no good for salon guests to come in only to leave and never come back to see you.

Lacey did the only thing she knew to do, which was hire a coach. The transformation that took place over the next month was unbelievable! The entire salon's pre-book percentage rose to 75%. To this day, most of our guests not only book one future appointment, but multiple ones spaced out over the next few months. Sometimes things happen and then you have to put in the work to update the schedule, but it's your business, so handle things the way that makes the most sense for you. If you're really organized and want to plan out your whole year around vacations and stuff like that, then by all means, go for it. Guaranteeing our income is vital because every month, you have bills to pay.

The coach was Randy Kunkel, whom we introduced back in Chapter 2. He asked Lacey how she was asking guests to book, and she informed him that each guest got asked to pre-book their next appointment before they left. He said, "Well, you're giving them the option to say no. So don't give them the option to say no. Stop asking and start telling." She immediately changed her verbiage to be more decisive. For example, let's say Jane came in on a Monday at six o'clock. You might say, "Jane, are Mondays at six going to work for you going forward? Or is there a better time we should look into?" Ask high vibrational questions that they can answer directly, and continuously follow up with both new and returning guests.

Someone who's been loyal to you for twenty years is, in our opinion, more valuable than someone who just walked in last week. So, follow up with every single guest, especially if you've done something new. This also just lets them know that you're thinking about them. You can schedule a follow-up appointment or even pass along a hairstyle you saw and thought would look good on them. People want to know that others care about them and that they matter. We might send a simple text message now, but back in the day, we used to write handwritten thank-you notes. After all, it's nice to get a piece of mail that's actually pleasant. There are companies out there that actually pay people to write handwritten notes.

Six-Figure Stylists diversify their income. You can do this through add-on services and maintaining a high service-to-client ratio. In other words, do more with what you have in your books. How many services do you typically do per client? Think about all of the things that you could have offered them during previous appointments, then ask yourself why you didn't. And if you feel like you are all out of add-on services, there are always classes you can attend to learn new ones. Go learn something that you can bring to your business and capitalize on.

A lot of salons now open as boutiques, but while that can also translate into having more overhead, it's a great way to increase profits. If the stylists like the clothing you offer, let them wear it to work and advertise it that way. You can have impulse buys like satin pillowcases or bonnets to sleep in, especially if you offer hair extensions. Stock up on ponytail holders, clips, brushes, and high-quality tools. If you don't have room for them in the physical space, post links to where your customers can find them online. Kylie's salon had a boutique after she consulted with the owner of I Speak Boutique, Brooke Santos. Brooke was a master at retail and merchandising, and after you've been in business for a while, you learn to seek out expert advice rather than wasting time figuring things out on your own.

"The more you learn, the more you earn."
– Robert T. Kiyosaki

Every time we learn a new skill, technique, product, or strategy, we gain a new resource to help us earn more. Education can never be taken away. Most people will do the same things as their parents, but if you want to do better than they did, you have to do something different.

"The key to financial freedom and great wealth is a person's ability or skill to convert earned income into passive income."
– Robert T. Kiyosaki

Explore passive income streams as well. Lacey was raised to believe that if she wanted something, she had to work hard for it. This is what's called a paradigm: a philosophical framework from which theories and generalizations form. She learned this after hiring her life coach, Mr. Bill, who helped her to see that you have to recognize and release these ingrained beliefs before you can replace them. The basis of her new paradigm is, "It feels good to make so much more money and work so much less."

Affiliate marketing, in our opinion, is the new retail. There are ways to streamline the process to where you can make money while you sleep or focus on things that you believe in and are actually passionate about. Do your research and find out what is on trend or what's projected to grow in your industry and find out how to capitalize on that. One way is to have affiliate products. There are sites that can get you hooked up with different affiliate links for free. Maybe you like to work out a lot, and the clients you've met at the gym all comment on how cute your workout clothes are. Become an affiliate for workout clothing. If people are commenting on physical changes you've made to your body, there's nothing wrong with becoming an affiliate for the nutrition products that you use. Lacey did all of those without having to sacrifice time and attention at home to do it. She shares how she did just this as a contributing author of *Purpose Driven Paycheck*. Learn to turn the everyday items you use into income-producing assets.

Six-Figure Stylist Takeaways:

- What does working smarter and not harder look like for you?
- Does your salon have systems in place to increase efficiency?
- Write down ways you can enhance your workflow systems to improve customer satisfaction and profits.
- What will you do with the raise you'll give yourself from working smarter?
- What steps do you need to take to prevent or recover from burnout?
- What policies can you implement now to establish healthy boundaries with your clients?
- Is there anyone you need to eliminate from your client list?
- Is it time to raise your prices? If so, take action now.
- What is your pre-book percentage, and what adjustments can you make to increase it?
- How can you diversify your income?
- What old paradigms need to be recognized, released, and replaced?

"**Bonus Resources**" **to enhance your experience.**

- *Purpose Driven Paycheck* book
- Breaking up with your salon guest

PLEASE SCAN THE QR CODE TO ACCESS:

Resources:

- *The Magic in Asking High Vibrational Questions* by Bill Mayer
- *Rich Dad Poor Dad: What the Rich Teach Their Kids About Money That the Poor and Middle Class Do Not!* by Robert T. Kiyosaki

CHAPTER 6

SO YOU WANT TO WORK FOR YOURSELF?

Building your own business from scratch can be a daunting task. However, there's nothing more rewarding than doing something ourselves.

Lacey learned about a month before she opened her salon that she'd already made mistakes. Had she figured it out sooner, she could have saved so much money and been so much more successful. Here are some things we would both do differently or have more consideration for if we'd known then what we do now.

1. Hire a coach as soon as you're able to—if you're able to.

Hire someone prior to creating the business plan who has been through it before so you don't make too many expensive mistakes early on. Doing so saves so much time and effort on things that shouldn't derail your plans, but can if you're not careful. As we mentioned in Chapter 1, coaches are so important.

Kylie hired a coach prior to opening her salon company, which saved her a lot of time and money. She started out with a business partner and was able to go to the Summit Salon Business Center in Tampa, Florida. There, she spent four whole days just absorbing as much information as she could. It was inspiring, exciting, terrifying, and even heartbreaking all at the same time. In a room filled with eighty different people, everyone has a story and an experience to share. There was hope, but also desperation. She and her partner were fortunate because they came only with big ideas, a vision of how they wanted their salon to operate, and what they wanted it to look like. For others, it was a last-ditch effort to pull their salon company out of its nosedive. Imagine an airplane headed straight for the ground. Kylie found this all truly gut-wrenching to witness.

One common thread she noticed, however, was that some of these people had run into their businesses blind, which is why most new businesses fail within the first two years of being open. They hadn't implemented budget guidelines, and some even admitted that they didn't know what breakevens were when they got started. On the other hand, some of the other attendees offered pure inspiration. Some salon owners there were running very successful companies, and some were even looking to open a second or third location. They shared what had helped make them extremely successful. In the midst of all of that, Kylie realized that she was there with a clean slate. Nothing was set in stone yet, and she was going in with an open mind.

To this day, she thinks that one of the most important hours of her life was the one spent with Randy Kunkel. Kylie remembers being so excited for that meeting; it was time to shine. She had everything planned out mostly in her mind but had also prepared a beautifully curated folder. Randy promptly threw it straight into the garbage. She was shocked; her blood, sweat, and tears went into that plan, and he'd just tossed her one copy. Randy said, "Do you want to make money or spend money?" Of course, she said she wanted to make money. For a couple of days, she'd listened to sob stories from those who hadn't. Then he said, "We've only got forty-five minutes, so I'm going to need you to listen up and write fast."

They discussed several things, including the importance of a good location and how much space would be allocated for retail and the actual stylist stations. In terms of the budget, she needed to figure out what she was willing to spend and where she was going to come up with that kind of money. Banks don't lend money to people based on big ideas and dreams; you'd better have a solid business plan when you approach a bank with your hand out. At the end of the hour, Randy recommended his own coach. A coach was a new concept to her at that time, but nowadays, it seems like there's a coach for everything. She hired a coach, secured a loan from the U.S. Small Business Administration (SBA), and managed to open her salon's doors in 2013—all thanks to the advice she received and the tools, tips, and tricks she learned along the way from great mentors. Owning a salon—or any company, for that matter—isn't easy. It is, however, worth it.

2. Invest wisely.

Do your research if you're planning to include a med spa or spa of some sort. A lot of the more expensive pieces of equipment can be rented, but do you have the proper training and certifications to operate it? Is your location properly zoned for the types of services that typically qualify as medical services? Sometimes this can take eight or nine weeks for the city to approve. Do you have a medical director on staff? What are the compliance requirements you need to adhere to in order to stay in business? Do you have the right insurance? Did you know that most salon insurance doesn't cover med spa services because they are much riskier? Will you be required to have an electronic medical record system (EMR)? If not, how are you planning to keep track of your patient files? Do you have standing operating protocols (SOP) in place? What requirements will your spa staff need to meet? These are just a few of the questions you'll want to ask yourself before investing in a spa operation.

3. Plan the salon's design carefully.

Know your square footage and space requirements, and open a smaller salon (less than 2,000 square feet) first. Spas take up so much space and are considered luxury services. In Lacey's experience, the smarter move is to build a salon business first—to test the waters a bit. The salon guests will give the data you need to know as to what to expect if you add cross-promotion for a spa in the mix. After all, salon clients and spa clients both want to look good and feel good.

The materials that will be used throughout the space are another important factor to consider. For example, as a new salon owner, Lacey chose the most beautiful cherry wood floors. They were a nightmare from day one. She'd tried to save money by having some friends help install them. This was also a mistake. They didn't know to remove the excess glue right away, so Lacey and her partner spent hours scraping the glue off with the help of harsh chemicals. Talk about blood, sweat, and tears! On top of that, dark floors show everything, and if you experience any flooding, they're ruined. You certainly shouldn't pay whoever handles the installation in full until the work is done; she learned this the hard way. In our experience, paying people up front led to a lack of incentive for them to finish the work. Lacey had a salon with unfinished paint and stain work, among other incomplete projects. She had to re-hire people or simply finish the jobs herself.

4. Hire slow, but fire fast.

Not everyone is going to be a great fit for your salon, but there's a bit of a learning curve to master at first. The more you vet people and fine-tune your interview process, the better you'll get. Our coaches always told us, "Hire the person, train the skill." You can always teach someone how to do hair, work the front desk, or handle any other position. You cannot, however, fix someone's personality. If someone isn't going to work out, don't drag it out. You're not doing anyone involved any favors. What you permit, you promote, so hire *slow*, but fire *fast*. When Lacey was a salon owner, she hired her friend Steph, who was then habitually late. Lacey would call her, worried that she was stranded on the side of the road or in a ditch somewhere, but she just kept oversleeping. She couldn't count on her, so Lacey had to fire her. She'd known this girl forever, but if she allowed that to continue, it would set an unwelcome standard among the rest of the staff. Kylie has certainly made the mistake of keeping unreliable employees in the hope that they could change their ways. This is part of being human, and often we want something more for someone than they want for themselves.

Be aggressive during the hiring stage. Salons everywhere will tell you that it's hard to hire, and in our experience, it is! Gone are the days of hiring anyone who walks through the door. Now, you have to offer more. It's also hard for stylists and beauty professionals to find a good place to work. We have recruited from cosmetology schools, taken out ads, and used social media, and still, we had times when we wondered where all the qualified people who wanted to work were. How are you going to attract stellar stylists? Offer what others aren't. Think outside the box. Rethink your hiring scripts and the questions you ask in the interviews. Minimum wage and commissions won't cut it anymore because the cost of living keeps rising. Hiring people on a 1099 basis when they don't have a client base is also happening everywhere, and it's maddening.

5. Know your budgeting basics.

You have to figure out how to work your finances as a business owner. It is different being a salon owner versus a suite renter or an employee. It is also different if you're renting a booth versus renting a suite. So, know where your money's going as well as where it's coming from, when it's coming in, and what the value of each client is. We are artists, but we also are running a business, and at some point, you need to understand effective budgeting guidelines. There are formulas you can use to figure it all out. If you don't, you'll find yourself overspending time and time again, which eats at your bottom line.

6. Create a positive salon culture.

Know the type of salon culture you want to perpetuate. Salon culture encompasses many things. For example, does your salon team use a code of honor? In the absence of rules, people tend to make up their own. You don't want your stylists all playing the same game but implementing different rules. In any type of business, you want things to be crystal clear. In Kylie's experience, most disagreements among staff and employers stem from unclear terms. Getting a group of like-minded individuals on the same page is the first step to setting your team up to run like a well-oiled machine.

While our coach recommended having everyone wear all black to promote unity and professionalism in the salon, this is one of those things Lacey feels differently about now. She was so young and serious about the success of her salon that she did everything she was told to do. She knew other salons had similar requirements. However, after working in a salon where she had the freedom to wear whatever she wanted (as long as it was still professional), she felt happier. She no longer had to wear only black clothes, and it was nice to get to express herself a bit more. She also noticed that most of the stylists at that salon dressed very casually. After Lacey moved to Texas, she worked in a salon that had a stricter dress code and noticed a shift in her mood. She didn't like not being able to wear her favorite clothes, and she didn't feel as dressy. At Kylie's salon, as long as they are dressed appropriately and their hair and makeup are done before they arrive for work, stylists have some freedom with what they wear.

7. Be flexible with the schedule.

You have to be able to keep the people who work for you happy. This means letting them have more control of their own schedules. When you're a salon owner, you've put everything on the line for that business in order to provide income for yourself and everybody who works with and for you. So, it's not just about being lenient or acting as their friend, but about being their understanding boss. It's hard to tell someone they can't have a specific day off; you want to be flexible, but you also have to have people there to keep your place running. In Kylie's salon, she has always allowed her employees to take off when needed for the sake of work-life balance, but only if the appropriate coverage is available. For example, Saturdays are busy, so she only allows two employees at a time to take Saturdays off.

8. Maintain professional boundaries.

We've all heard the saying, "It's not personal; it's just business." One thing we've learned operating salon companies is how to be professional and set boundaries. It's natural to want to be everyone's friend, but in doing so, you'd be setting yourself up for heartache. Not everyone is meant to stay with one company their entire life, and even the people who you think are your best friends may eventually move on.

9. Offer better base salaries and benefits.

After all, you want to attract top-tier talent. Basic education offerings aren't cutting it anymore; stylists need awesome educational opportunities, and they want to be sent to exciting places. Kylie's salon is loyal to the brands Redken and Pureology. Why, you ask? Being loyal to a brand often means it will go above and beyond to support the continued education of your stylists. Her salon achieved Redken Black Level status after being open less than eighteen months. This opened the door to phenomenal support from the brand. Soon, artists flowed in to offer amazing educational opportunities for the staff. Stay on top of industry trends. Help them get certified in high-ticket services so they can earn more. Give them a photoshoot or fashion week opportunities. Have regular events that the stylists want to be a part of and are excited to help promote. A lack of benefits isn't attractive, but it's all too common. There needs to be a shift in the industry; beauty school graduates deserve to make fair wages and enjoy basic benefits at the very least.

10. Create a structured business plan.

In beauty school, they don't teach you how to start a limited liability company (LLC), how to obtain your Employer Identification Number (EIN), how to file a "doing business as" (DBA) or trade name, how to get your seller's permit, or what city and state licensing you need to have. As a business owner, there are a lot of things you need to do to get started. But, if you're an employee or you want to rent, there's a different list of things that you need to have.

If you work for yourself, you make 50% on your commissions. It's different when you have to pay for everything related to the business. Learn how to set those things up on your own or have a professional help you. Getting a business bank account and different merchant accounts, getting a domain and website name, finalizing your taxes correctly, managing expenses, and establishing your referral program: none of these things are taught, but they're all essential for a successful business. Are you sending out automated emails? Is mass texting available to you? What kind of software do you use? What's your marketing plan? Have you outsourced your website design and maintenance, or are you handling that in-house? At the end of this chapter, we have a resource for you to help with websites, mass emailing, and mass texting.

11. Start with the end in mind.

When most of us start our beauty careers, we don't think about the endgame. We get so wrapped up in and excited about the glitz, the glamor, and huffing endless hairspray. We rarely think about how we are going to successfully retire. Have you considered passive income streams you can work with while you're still behind the chair? Do you have other types of investments in mind that can yield high interest? This takes some financial literacy and planning, and most of us don't think about it until it's too late. How many stylists do you know that have successfully planned for retirement?

All of this is why we are both so passionate about helping other beauty professionals and have created Beauty Concierge (our new membership site—get access by scanning the QR code at the end of this chapter), which includes ongoing education and personalized coaching based on what they've learned along the way, what they've invested in, and how they feel they could have done it even better. We all have dreams, whether it's to own our own salon and/or spa or to work for ourselves. Beauty school teaches the skills stylists need to make money, but they don't teach you everything you need to thrive in the industry. The things we're sharing in the pages of this book and in our courses address these vital gaps.

Six-Figure Stylist Takeaways:

- Hire a coach as soon as you're able to.
- Invest wisely.
- Plan the salon's design carefully.
- Hire slow, but fire fast.
- Know your budgeting basics.
- Create a positive salon culture.
- Be flexible with the schedule.
- Maintain professional boundaries.
- Offer better base salaries and benefits.
- Create a structured business plan.
- Start with the end in mind.

"Bonus Resources" to enhance your experience.

- Hiring scripts
- Example of a team code of honor
- MyGeniusLeads
- Free Beauty Concierge Lounge Community

PLEASE SCAN THE QR CODE TO ACCESS:

CHAPTER 7

INVESTING IN YOURSELF

Never stop learning. We feel that continual learning is equivalent to the growth of the soul.

Six-Figure Stylists continuously put conscious effort into their professional development. Twenty-three years ago, we had to physically go get educated. Lacey traveled across the nation to learn new things and get additional certifications. She attended as many local seminars as possible at the start of her career when she realized she didn't know half of what she thought she did when she finished school. Just prior to opening her salon, she flew to Salt Lake City to learn more about cellulite reduction and microdermabrasion since she'd purchased a machine for these procedures for her spa. Then, she flew to Tampa to visit the Summit Salon Business Center, only to learn that the $26,000 cellulite reduction and microderm machine, along with the $40,000 laser and the Vichy capsule, were all very expensive mistakes. Let's just say she learned some very good lessons on business, due diligence, and discernment and shares them so that others don't have to learn the hard way like she did.

She continued her business education by attending two phases of the Summit Salon Business Center's business training sessions for salon owners. She didn't stop there but went to multiple sessions with Front Desk Doctor, Kristy Valenzuela, the industry leader in maximizing front desk earnings and training one's salon staff. She attended associate program training so she wouldn't have to reinvent the wheel when it came to effectively training associates. Next, she attended merchandising and retail classes with Peter Millard, who is known for helping companies maximize retail profits through displays, after she read his book *Reinventing Space: The Clear Logic to Successful Salon Design and Retail Merchandising*.

Her first trip to the Redken Exchange (the number one education center for our industry) was actually thanks to a ticket she won in a raffle while attending a class at the St. Louis Discover hair show in 2006. This ticket was worth thousands, and she felt she was destined to win it. She took her first associate, Steph, with her to the Big Apple. Steph worked so hard to pay for that trip; they both saved their tips for more than six months just to afford it. It would be Lacey's first time in NYC and Steph's first time on a plane. The week before they were scheduled to go, Lacey suddenly came down with an illness and had to be hospitalized. Her doctor did not want her to go, but after making her promise to take her medical records and follow a special diet, along with passing on information for the hospitals near where she would be, he released her the night before they took off. There was no way she was missing this class.

The class, taught by Sam Villa and Kris Sorbie, was all about advanced cutting and coloring. NYFW was going on at the same time, and Kris was styling hair there. Lacey and Stephanie were in awe. Styling at NYFW was a distant dream for Lacey then, but she decided that if Kris could do it, then she could too. The whole experience was life-changing. She learned new ways to cut from Sam, new ways to color, how to achieve a seamless ombre look before it became popular, and new ways to educate her associates. She was inspired by the city, the people, the fashion, and the architecture. She even bumped into friends she had met while she was in Tampa the previous year. She had found her place and knew that she was going to become a Redken Artist. Lacey also decided that she was going to work with Sam and Kris while she was there.

It was after this trip that she told her husband (at the time) her plans for the future. You know, the one who didn't want her to get her hopes up? But Lacey's a firm believer that when you make a decision and have faith that it will be done, God has a way of working it out. A few years later, while sitting down to lunch together in Albuquerque, Lacey shared that story with Sam, who had become not only a great mentor but a friend. While she has had many mentors, Sam is truly the best educator she has had the privilege of learning from and with. He showed her that there's a lesson in everything, even when you go to eat or attend a ball game. He taught her how he did things like setting himself up for success, organizing his workspace, and adjusting lighting and seating. He taught her to anticipate what he would need so she could have it ready before he even asked.

This prepared her to be able to do the same when her career advanced. He showed her that while everyone else is sleeping, successful people are practicing new skills like becoming ambidextrous. He would say things like, "Now take this, and make it your own. Share this as your own. You teach this now." It turns out that the most famous educator in our industry is also the most humble person. He led by example and told Lacey that he believed in her—that she could do great things. He taught her how to create value not only behind the chair but in the classroom, on stage, or wherever you find yourself. He takes innovation to an unthinkable level, so after attending his class, if she was in a tight spot, she would always ask herself, *What would Sam do?*

When she auditioned to become a certified Redken Artist, she had to send in a physical portfolio. Presentation was everything, so she hired a videographer friend to help her with her audition video. His work made her talent stand out, which just goes to show that you should never be afraid to outsource to someone who is better than you at something. Next, she had three separate weeks of Redken Artist Induction in Tampa to look forward to, which Lacey paid for using part of the small inheritance she received from her mom's life insurance policy. She wanted the money to mean something so her mom's legacy would go on forever. That's the beautiful thing about education; it can never be taken away, and it's meant to be shared.

She was surprised to learn that when they hired her as an artist, she was considered an independent contractor, not a trainee. They set everyone up with a roommate at the hotel and bussed them each day to The Salon Professional Academy. They sent instructions on what to bring and what to wear, and that's when Lacey started learning about dressing to impress. She borrowed clothes from a friend because she had just lost thirty pounds and all of her money was going to this training. The first night, there was a meet and greet; she was excited and a little nervous since she was still very guarded. The first week was all about product knowledge and getting their feet wet in facilitation. The next phase was focused on color and more facilitation, and the final phase covered design, finishing, and more facilitation. Each phase also contained personal development segments.

The training was intense and lasted all day. Each night, Lacey had homework. Sr. Director of Training at L'Oreal John Stellato described it as the equivalent of Navy Seal training for hair artists and educators, and they were not kidding. There were lots of tears, and everything had to be perfect. Lacey learned how to do things frontward, backward, sideways—you name it. Each time she went back, it just got better. She got to know herself better, and it was truly one of the best experiences of her life. During this time, she gained the courage and confidence she needed to end her first marriage. She made great friends with whom she is still in touch to this day, and she definitely got more than what she bargained for. She actually met her current husband at the wedding of one of her new friends years later.

After the summer, she began Redken Artist Connection (RAC). It's annual training (sometimes twice a year) for all certified Redken Artists who want to keep up with the latest trends, products, and innovation. Each session consisted of technical skills labs, personal development seminars, and facilitation demos. Her first RAC trip was to Scottsdale, Arizona. Every other year, they host International RAC sessions, and artists fly in from all over the world, usually to Las Vegas. It was amazing to be reunited with everyone that she learned from before, and Lacey and some of her friends were starstruck. The energy was incredible; there was such a high vibe throughout the event. It was honestly hard when it came time to leave this vibration behind.

The training sessions occur both during the day and the night, and you're surrounded by a few hundred of the most talented and like-minded beauty professionals in the world the entire time. Suddenly, she realized she was one of them. She did the same things they all did to get in those rooms and hold the positions they did, and they were all people, just putting their pants on every morning like everybody else. It truly was a dream come true, but dreams don't come true by chance. They come to fruition through hard work, intention, sacrifice, and determination. Other than her talents, Lacey had two other key things going for her: hunger and desperation. She was hungry for success; she needed it like air. She was desperate for it and willing to do whatever it took.

After she chose to specialize in color treatments, Lacey became a Redken Certified Haircolorist. She studied for six months to pass the test and actually had to borrow money from her dad to attend; she had spent everything she had on her education and a divorce that left her with only $300 to her name that ended up getting stolen during a break-in, plus two foreclosed homes. But she would stop at nothing to achieve her goal. The day before the test, she met a friend in NYC, where they stayed with another hairdresser friend in Brooklyn to save money. The night before the test, they each had to lug three suitcases, their backpacks, tripods, and coats through the streets of Brooklyn to the subway. No car services would take them as far as the site of the mock test; talk about planes, trains, and automobiles! The next day featured an essay and multiple choice test, then an intense practical exam. Between testing sessions, Lacey met more new friends, some of whom she would later run into at various hair shows across the country or even work with. The hair world is a small world, after all.

Lacey took several classes at the Redken Exchange, including a corrective color seminar, and traveled to Las Vegas every other year for the Redken Symposium, which is the largest hair show in the world. Working there was such a valuable experience, as was learning from the other artists and observing the attendees who came to learn. It was so rewarding and fulfilling. Truthfully, it had to be because the money one is paid to work a show doesn't add up to the amount you might earn just teaching a class. The shows pay more in terms of what you learn and how much credibility you build. Lacey had to retrain her brain in this regard. Working a show is almost like advertising, and it's a lot of work. Model calls usually started at five or six in the morning. They would usually work the shows into the evenings, then, depending on what they needed to prep for the next day, might have to stay until ten or eleven at night.

After that, there were nightly events to attend. She often brought her evening attire to the model call in the morning because there wasn't time to go back to where she was staying to change before the nighttime events. Showing up, not to mention how you show up, to those matters. She might get back at one or two in the morning just to get up again at four. That's "show life." She wanted it badly and is so very grateful for that part of her life.

In Tampa, she also attended social media training sessions for businesses. She checked out Micheal Cole's programs multiple times and in various places to learn how to step up her business. These classes were so impactful, and she learned more each time she went. Lacey has also done one-on-one hair extension workshops in Louisville to perfect her bonding skills and earned other certifications like beaded and hand-tied extension methods in St. Louis. She began sharing some of the most valuable tips in her own classes and with the staff at her salon. Lacey got certified to facilitate L'Oreal's Salon Emotion program and even started getting more education online in between various Redken educational opportunities and masterclasses with Chris Baran and Chris Moody.

Luckily, she was used to online education formats, and because she saw the future in it, she set up an in-home studio mere months before COVID-19 sent everyone into lockdown so she could start facilitating her own online events. During the year in which in-person events were canceled, Lacey got certified to facilitate live, hands-on workshops for Redken. It was so incredible to be able to empower people from home with the skills they need to succeed. While Lacey had to spend money to travel around the country, stylists could now spend less money and still get an incredible learning experience. Lacey still prefers in-person education herself. Just last year, she went to Alabama for a one-on-one, two-day avant-garde workshop with Sabrena Handley, one of the most talented and skilled avant-garde artists in the country. She has learned that when you want something, you just have to go for it. If you don't ask for what you want, you'll likely never get it.

> "Ask and ye shall receive; seek, and you shall find; knock, and the door shall be opened to you."
> – (Luke 11:9)

Lacey has had the privilege of traveling to different salons across the nation and sharing everything that has been passed down to her. We believe that when you learn something that changes your life or you cultivate a gift or talent, then you must share it. That's one of the main reasons why we are sharing these things with you.

Kylie has traveled to multiple cities over the years for extensive training on extensions, as well as to continue her own education. Almost two years ago, she visited Las Vegas and discovered a new hair extension company called Hair Lingerie. Its product helped her cut her application time way down, and she quickly discovered that it was truly the best product on the market.

"One of the things I learned from my mentors was to look for the hole in the blanket. Most people look at the hole in the blanket as the blanket is damaged. I was taught to look beyond the obvious. The hole in the blanket is a void waiting to be filled. As I looked around the hair industry, specifically the hair extensions industry, there was no way to apply extensions that did not damage the client's natural hair over time. There was no quick method of installing extensions and there was no company mentoring stylists to be more successful in their own business. This is why I invented tape-in extensions and started Hair Lingerie.

> *"Always look for the hole in the blanket."*
> –Kiara Bailey, creator of Hair Lingerie

If any of you do hair extensions, you know this is huge because the process can take hours otherwise. This little learning trip led Kylie to do almost half a million dollars behind her chair in 2023, all while maintaining a shorter workweek and going through treatment for breast cancer. The thing was, Kylie wasn't necessarily looking for a new brand of extensions; after all, she had been using another brand for many years and was a master at individual keratin extensions. Hair Lingerie found her thanks to the Instagram algorithm—or maybe the hair gods. Either way, Hair Lingerie's unique mentorship program, regular check-ins, and unparalleled customer service quickly drew her in. It was evident from the beginning that Kiara actually cares for the stylists and wants to celebrate their success. In fact, Kylie just received an ambassador award!

During one of the visits that Kiara paid Kylie at the salon, Kylie made a point to tell her this is what sets her company apart. The other extension company Kylie had used for more than twenty years *never* checked in. Hair Lingerie is built on integrity, both in regard to the stylists using it and the clients wearing it. Not only that, but she has also now created a hair care line called ONLY, which consists of a shampoo, conditioner, and oil. It's an insurance policy, if you will, for the clients investing in the hair of their dreams!

In addition to in-person classes, there are a plethora of online or digital courses available and ready for consumption. There's YouTube, TikTok, and so many other platforms to explore. If you're in a commission-based salon, you're probably blessed enough to have educators come in regularly, especially if the salon owner is visibly loyal to a brand. Recall that when you're loyal to a brand, there's always the possibility that it will send educators to your salon so they can teach different sales or application techniques. Stay on top of whatever is hot in the current season. You have to continue to not only keep up with the trends but also learn to forecast them.

Let people know what you're learning, what you are excited about, and what kind of work you want to be doing for your clients as a result. When Lacey learned "ombre" and color-melting techniques, she couldn't wait to bring them back to her clients. She sent a press release out to the local papers, and while she wasn't on social media at the time, she did share her excitement with those who sat in her chair. She even let them know about it prior to their appointments to build their anticipation. She set up a mannequin and photos in the salon so people could see her work and decide if they wanted something similar. She taught her coworkers what she had learned, and soon, they were all modeling the trend.

Fast-forward a couple of years to when ombre finally hit the Midwest. Lacey promoted her know-how on social media alongside photos of the looks she was creating. People started calling to book with her for these services after they saw the look and learned that if they wanted to jump on that trend, she was their go-to stylist. This was how she branded herself. Her clients still sit down and say, "I want the latest." Then, she asks them to refer their friends to her.

Kylie has also invested in personal branding. One look at her social media accounts, and there is no confusion as to what her specialty is, what kinds of clients she is attracting, and how this all converts to appointments and sales. In the salon, there are extension brochures and displays everywhere. New guests ask what's up with the hair pieces hanging all over the place and *boom!*—the conversation has started, and it's time to educate a client about a service they may want to try out.

Six-Figure Stylists are certified in different types of extensions for added versatility and so they can do a total hair transformation anytime. You can make somebody feel like a million bucks by giving them their dream hair without the pesky time it takes to grow it naturally. We both specialize in styling the kind of hair that some people would never have if left to their own devices. Whether this is due to genetics, hormonal imbalances, or thyroid-related issues, there are so many solutions we can now offer people who don't love their hair because they can't seem to get the length and volume they want. When you experience the magic of dream hair for yourself, you know exactly how your clients are going to feel, and you won't be able to wait to get started. We also refer to this as power hair. Power hair makes you feel like you can do anything. It helps people walk more confidently and feel like their most beautiful selves.

You can get certified in hair color, balayage, curls, corrective color, and so much more. This shows both current and potential clients that you're serious about your career and not just another hobby hairstylist. Figure out what it is that you need financially and what skills you want to learn, then set aside time to plan out your educational endeavors for the next year. Lacey traveled the country for thirteen years as an educator and knows that salons and beauty brands are starting to plan their events for the next year around August. So, by October, she would already know her schedule for the whole next year. Without education, sales taper off, and let's not forget that no sales = no income. You don't have to be part of a big company to plan out educational events; even if you work in a smaller salon, provide some on your own. The best part is that there is never a shortage of new things to learn—you just have to get out there and do it!

Our professional licenses get printed in the exact same manner as those of doctors, lawyers, and dentists. We are valuable, and it's time to take charge and get serious about your chosen profession. One of Kylie's favorite sayings came from a mentor of hers: "If it's meant to be, it's up to me!" Let that soak in for a minute. If you don't like something about your career or want better for yourself, it's up to you. And the kicker is that if nothing changes, there's no one else to blame. We can reinvent ourselves at any given time. Who we *were* does not have to be who we *are*.

In addition to the many classes you can choose from, there's a multitude of personal development resources out there. We're big advocates for *The Ultimate Wayne Dyer Library*. This was life-changing for us, and we know it will be for you. He talks about our mindset and how we can protect our energy. To do that, we have to be able to recognize when to reset it. If you don't, the world and its troubles will eat you alive. You have to get to a place in which you know your worth, your value, and what's important to you versus what's not. Consider what you need to let go of, whether it's people, things, words, energy, or even thoughts.

> "When you change the way you look at things,
> the things you look at change."
> –Wayne Dyer

We cannot control other people, only how we respond to them, and all we have is the present. When we dwell on the past, we relive what we have gone through, but we can't change what has happened, only the way we look at it. Every single thing in this life happens for us, not to us. If you have this attitude of gratitude, you can begin to find peace and understand that what happens in our lives is a result of our own thoughts. Wayne's teachings helped us take our power back by not letting other people's thoughts or opinions affect our moods, energy levels, or vibration. Everyone's entitled to and responsible for their own thoughts, but when we put emphasis on what others think, Wayne refers to this as EGO, or "edging God out." Choose peace or choose your ego. Be one with our creator, or whatever higher power you subscribe to, be grateful for the life you have. It was given to you for a reason.

> *"So God created man in his own image, in the image of God He created him; male and female He created them."*
> *– (Genesis 1:27)*

Another great resource is *The Magic of Thinking Big* by David J. Schwartz. This book is fantastic, but we especially like its second chapter, which introduces the idea of "excusitis," or the tendency to make excuses. Kylie attended a class in Las Vegas, where they spoke about this chapter. That day, the educator challenged her way of thinking, but the information was so valuable. She had every excuse not to get on that plane since she was in the middle of chemo treatments but chose to invest in herself and have a great time. Ironically, the first form of "excusitis" listed in the book is, "But my health isn't good." After reading that paragraph, she realized she never used cancer as an excuse. Getting well, having a positive mindset, and moving forward was her focus, not the disease itself. She purchased the book, highlighted that section, and still reads it every week per the educator's recommendation. The chapter it's in touches on the four main types of "excusitis:" *health, intelligence, age,* and *luck*. The truth is we can all find a reason to lay blame elsewhere, but this book can help its readers recognize this thought pattern and change.

We also recommend reading *Think and Grow Rich* by Napoleon Hill. One of our favorite quotes from this book is, "Only those who become 'money-conscious' ever accumulate great riches." Money consciousness means that the mind has become so thoroughly saturated with the desire for money that you can already envision yourself in possession of it.

> *"Weak desires bring weak results, just as a small amount of fire makes a small amount of heat. If you find yourself lacking in persistence, this weakness may be remedied by building a stronger fire under your desires."*
> *– Napoleon Hill*

This book also provides an exact blueprint for how to get rich. Napoleon warns that those who do not follow these instructions will surely fail. One of the things he teaches is to write out our goals. Let's say you want to gain $21 million by a specific date. You would detail how you intend to come into possession of this money and what you intend to do with it on paper. Read it aloud, and affirm it for yourself at least twice daily.

If personal development is important to you, you should dedicate at least ten minutes a day to it. Reading *The 15 Invaluable Laws of Growth* by John C. Maxwell is another great place to start.

> *"You will never change your life until you change something you do daily. Small disciplines repeated with consistency every day lead to great achievements gained slowly over time."*
> – John C. Maxwell

Small things do, in fact, add up over time. Lacey remembers when she decided to start eating healthier and making her overall health a priority first thing every day. Day one didn't go as planned, but she got there by forming daily habits and cultivating consistency that became her lifestyle over time. The same is true for bad habits. We encourage you to take a moment and think about one thing you could do to improve your daily life. What bad habit is holding you back? We make it a quarterly practice to evaluate our life and daily habits. If there is something we're doing that isn't serving us, it must go.

We also brainstorm new, positive daily habits to start off each quarter. That way, when we look back over the year, we can see exactly what we have done to improve the quality of our lives. For example, Lacey just started cold plunging. She started out at three minutes for three days a week, then built up to doing it every day. She will continue reminding herself to do this until she no longer has to think about it because it's simply part of her lifestyle. Maybe you need to drink more water; set a goal and monitor yourself daily until you no longer need to. It could be walking a certain distance or spending time in prayer or meditation. Think about what you really want in life because everything is energy, and everything we do or even think either pushes us closer to our goals or pulls us away from them.

These are all just suggestions for balancing your life and for holistic development. We have to do that as beauty professionals; we come across too much energy not to. We find it so valuable to clear our minds before we go spend an entire day with people and again after the workday ends.

Lacey once had a salon guest named "Sharon" who was miserable. She would complain about her narcissistic, abusive husband during every single visit, although she had no intention of leaving him. She just needed a safe place to let go of that energy. Lacey learned to listen with an empathetic ear, and at the end of each appointment, Sharon would say, "I feel like I should be paying you extra for all the therapy." Lacey calls it "hairapy." After Sharon left, Lacey felt so drained and negative that she would need to go outside and recharge her energy. Sometimes, she'd seek solitude and do some breathing exercises. Other times, she would listen to some high-vibe music and do jumping jacks or run around the parking lot behind the salon. She knew she couldn't carry this energy, especially because Sharon was almost always her first guest of the day. If you have a guest like this, see if you can book that person at the end of your day. In Sharon's case, that didn't work, so Lacey found ways to cope and recharge.

Even if you're running behind, take a minute and do this as needed, even if it's just a quick method of physically shaking off negative energy. Lacey also prays over her guests during scalp massages and often uses Reiki massage techniques. She regularly prays over herself and her home with anointing oil just to be on the safe side.

According to Joanna Beck, founder of Joanna Beck Ministries, one way to pray over your mind is to touch your forehead with anointing oil (which you can purchase through the organization or make on your own) and say:

"I break every mind-breaking spirit off of my life now in the name of Jesus. I command the power of witchcraft to be broken over me. I command every lie and false decree to be broken. I command all mental oppression to go from me now! I command every mind-binding spirit to lose me and go now in the name of Jesus. I think 'God' thoughts. I dream 'God' dreams. I imagine Godly imaginations. According to Philippians 2:5, I have the mind of Christ. I am saturated in peace and protection. I have a sound mind. I am free from the spirit of fear, in Jesus's name. I am free! Father, I thank you for your love, peace, and freedom. I worship you and praise you and declare a free mind now in the name of Jesus Christ. Amen."

If you attend a class and find that you want to learn more, raise your vibration before you dive into any independent study. Each Redken educational event starts with what we call "Energy." We play a high-vibe song and have attendees clap along and follow the educator's movements. Clapping and high fives raise vibrations and create synchronicity. It's a great state change, especially after lunch. Lacey even helped some of her former salon teams adopt this process prior to starting a shift. It really promotes teamwork, joy, and laughter—all of which, you'll recall, live on the same frequency as money.

You have to invest in your physical health. As beauty professionals, our income is just as dependent on our physical health as it is on our mental well-being. If we're putting crap in our bodies, our bodies will feel like crap. We have to take care of our hands, feet, knees, back, and joints. We can't properly take care of our clients if we don't take care of ourselves. "Health is wealth" is not just a clever saying. So, you have to make time for your health on a daily basis.

One aspect of this is embarking on your physical fitness journey if you haven't done so already. About six years ago, after her daughter was born, Lacey started using a nutrition company as the basis of her diet. This investment changed her entire life. It made her look into the science of nutrition and start to develop a healthier lifestyle. She once again felt comfortable in her own skin; as an added bonus, every pound we lose takes four pounds of pressure off our knees. (Source: arthritis.org.) These changes in diet got her thinking, and she realized that everything she was putting into her body was either healing or hurting her.

So, she began to look at her health and wellness in a much different way and started working out more intentionally. She wasn't just going to the gym and zoning out on a treadmill. She went for walks, which, if you're just starting out with a more regular exercise routine, is not a bad idea. However, she also spent more time focusing on the different muscle groups. She highly recommends doing a lower body day, an upper body day, a core day, and a stretch or Pilates day just to give your muscles a slight break. Try different classes, and make time for different types of workouts that you actually enjoy doing. Going to fitness classes can introduce you to other people who have similar interests, and exercise, in general, releases endorphins that make you happy, so working out can make you a much happier person in general. When we exercise regularly, we also have a tendency to eat better and be a lot more mindful of what we're putting in our bodies; plus, it helps clear our heads.

To this day, Lacey still uses the same superfood nutrition system. Protein pacing combined with cleansing days keeps her organs clear of toxins. Each day, she has at least one plant-based protein shake, sometimes two, along with mostly organic fruits and vegetables, plus nuts. She never misses greens, collagen, or adaptogens. Adopting this same approach could mean spending as much as $500 each month on nutrition, and yes, it can feel like a lot if you're not used to spending that much at the grocery store. So, you have to change your mindset about what you're putting in your body and how.

Lacey believes in being able to have what you want because when you eliminate things or tell yourself you can't have something, you tend to want it more. Eating this way helped heal her stomach problems after having her gallbladder removed in her early twenties. She'd felt sick every day for more than fifteen years, but this system helped her learn more about what her body likes and what she should avoid. She believes that if we ingest the foods that God put on this earth for us to eat, we will be healthy. After all, He is a great physician. Everything we need is here for us.

We've all been in a position where we are not very happy with our bodies, and there's nothing worse than not liking yourself in or out of clothes. We've heard people say nothing tastes as good as skinny feels, but for us, it's not about being skinny; it's about loving our amazing bodies and being confident in our own skin. It's about loving ourselves enough to make the time to improve our health. We've said it for years, but the better you look, the better you feel. When you feel better, you carry yourself more confidently. If you're not happy with the way you look and you're uncomfortable in your clothes, it can be harder for you to do quality hair. So, invest time in a gym membership and a good nutrition system. We promise you, it's just as, if not less expensive than fast food, and way less expensive than constantly being sick.

Kylie tried training at a garage bodybuilder gym with no air conditioning or heat. She worked hard with a fantastic trainer three to four days a week, and each day, they focused on different muscle categories. It made her focus on developing better eating habits; after all, there wasn't much point in devoting so much time and sweat to her physical well-being if she was just going to eat the same unhealthy crap. As the saying goes, you can't train away a bad diet, and if you're boozing, you aren't losing. Once you embrace this attitude, you'll see the physical shifts happening on a whole other level. Clients started noticing and mentioning her sculpted shoulders and arms. They always asked if it was because we use our arms to blow dry hair all day. Not quite—hours of torture in the gym and discipline got her there. And once these lifestyle changes become a habit, your body craves it.

A strong core and glutes will help prevent back issues down the road. Use anti-fatigue mats and buy good shoes that are made for standing all day and that you like; you may even consider a spare pair. After all, our feet have the responsibility of carrying all of our weight all day. Have a cutting stool that will allow you to get off your feet every once in a while. If you're skeptical regarding whether or not you'll be comfortable sitting while doing hair, just give it a try for your body's sake. Use ergonomic tools that will make it easier on your hands. They can only do so many cuts in a lifetime, just like your wrists can only turn so much.

It's imperative to invest in learning how to hold your body as well as your arms and wrists in such a way that you don't needlessly harm your body because when you depend on it for your income. You could become ambidextrous so you can use both hands to hold brushes, meaning one doesn't always have to assume less comfortable grips and positions than the other. You have to learn how to use both hands to hold the blow dryer and your irons and stand in different positions rather than just directly in front of the area that you're working on. This takes strategy, practice, and muscle memory. It took us years to figure it all out, but our shoulders, elbows, wrists, fingers, backs, feet, knees, and everything in between are thankful because of how well we do our jobs.

Six-Figure Stylists invest in themselves mentally, not just physically, but the two harmonize well. Create a space for yourself in which you can visualize the life that you want and reset your energy as needed. Don't think about things that you don't want to happen; see things as you want them to be. It's easy to let your mind drift while you visualize, but you have to set clear intentions if you want to see results. Lacey visualized owning her salon and spa, teaching, and being on stage. She visualized working with hair gurus she respected, the kind of work schedule she wanted, and the kind of money she wanted to earn. She visualized having her daughter and living on the beach. She even purchased a vibration plate with a fifteen-minute timer so she could visualize while increasing her vibration and working on her physical health. Kylie, on the other hand, visualized owning a salon and mentoring everyday stylists while providing them a great place to work and be creative. She visualized the money she wanted to make and what she wanted to do with it. She visualized her schedule and the days she would have more time with her family in her dream home. Let yourself daydream, and set aside time in your schedule for visualization exercises. In an occupation like ours, where we are used to bustling around all day, stopping for this practice may feel uncomfortable, but Sam Villa always once said, "Sometimes you have to slow down to speed up." Slow down long enough to see it all in your mind. When you perfect this practice and make it a daily habit, it will speed up the results you're chasing.

Six-Figure Stylists set themselves apart from others by being the queen (or king) bee in their salon. Every salon has a queen bee. It's the person you go to and say, "Hey, will you check out my guest? This is what she wants… what should I use on her?" Granted, if you don't know what to use on your own client, then you'd better take some time to brush up on your skills. If you are a hairstylist who does hair color but isn't grounded in color theory, you're likely going to spend a lot of time on redos. Get yourself into some classes and learn everything there is to know about color treatments, such as what is in, what and why you would use what to counteract what. You have to know these laws and principles, and yet it's shocking how many stylists don't truly understand color.

In most classes Lacey has facilitated, she's found that most people there just weren't grounded in the theory. Stop making excuses about why you can't use a certain color or have to put natural tones (N) in every formula. Stop blaming manufacturers for not providing quality products. Learn about dye molecules, the oxidative process, and what can happen (though not on a guest) when you add heat to chemicals that aren't designed to be used with heat. Know when to use color on wet hair. Don't ask someone else for their favorite formulas. It's called hair color formulation for a reason; each starting level is different. It will never look the same as someone else's color because it's not the same hair. You can't expect the same end result.

If you're in a suite, you may not have somebody you can ask questions, or you might have to run down the hallway to do so. But, if you're in a salon, no matter the layout or other different circumstances, we highly recommend gathering a supportive tribe that works well together. Teamwork helps build your confidence while you cultivate the knowledge you need to be able to formulate anything.

In beauty school, Lacey didn't understand why color theory was so important. She figured that if she wanted the end result to look like 6N, that's what she would use. It's just how she was taught. When she got out into the salon world, she was scared to death to try anything on the cool side of the color wheel. She wondered why they even included green, but keep in mind that this was the early 2000s when these trends weren't so mainstream. Thankfully, warm tones were trending, but she still had a big problem. She had a client who wanted to go from dark red to platinum blonde. When all was said and done, her hair turned out a lovely shade of bright orange, and Lacey didn't know how to fix it because she was too scared to use anything cool and didn't know the foundations of the color wheel. She ultimately lost the client but decided she had to learn color. She got herself into classes nearly every single week, only to discover that she didn't know about glazing or toning. She didn't know the rules or why she would need to put color on dry hair versus wet, or why color takes a certain amount of time to oxidize, or where color molecules live on or in strands of hair depending on how long it had been on. She didn't know about pre-toning and dye molecules or which types she needed to use, when, and why. The point is to invest in your education and become an expert in your craft. We all want successful careers so we can eventually retire.

Six-Figure Stylist Takeaways:

- When was the last time you personally had power hair?
- Create your education schedule for the rest of this year.
- In what ways can you invest in yourself?
- How are you investing in your personal development?
- What certification could take you to the next level in your career?
- Take at least one day every eight weeks and do something that brings you joy.

- What do you need to release in order to regain or reset your energy?
- What bad habit is holding you back that no longer serves you? How will you replace it?
- Take charge of your health; get started by listing one change you need to make and how you can incorporate it into your current routine.

"Bonus Resources" to enhance your experience.

- Beauty Concierge Blow Dry Boot Camp
- Isagenix nutrition
- Color Theory mini-course

PLEASE SCAN THE QR CODE TO ACCESS:

Resources:

- *The Ultimate Wayne Dyer Library* by Wayne Dyer
- *Think and Grow Rich* by Napoleon Hill
- *The 15 Invaluable Laws of Growth* by John C. Maxwell
- *The Magic of Thinking Big* by David J. Schwartz
- The Bible

CHAPTER 8

SMART FINANCIAL MANAGEMENT AND EXIT STRATEGIES

Unfortunately, we don't have a crystal ball. In life, what we can expect is the unexpected. With that in mind, we cannot stress enough how important planning for the future is: when you want to take a vacation, have a baby, buy your future home, or when you get older and want to retire, or what should happen if you or a loved one comes down with a serious illness. This is all part of smart financial management.

Everyone needs to recharge their batteries at some point. Yes, we're talking about vacation! Be proactive and plan for it, like setting up a savings account just for your future vacations and contributing to it every week. If you save $100 each week in tip money, that's $5,000 per year. Best of all, with it being in its own special account, you won't have easy access to it on a regular basis and can better ensure that you actually save the money. Most stylists don't realize that when they take a vacation, it directly affects your pre-booking for weeks to come. Six-Figure Stylists are mindful and strategic about getting those clients booked before they leave, knowing they'll have that business to look forward to when they return.

So you're ready to welcome home that bouncing bundle of joy? Let's talk about planning for maternity leave and how to balance motherhood with your career. First of all, it's never too late to start saving for a future family. Okay, maybe you're not planning to have kids, but you never know when things might change or when you're going to have to take time off work. Lacey was a successful stylist and platform artist when she got pregnant with her daughter at the age of thirty-five. Imagine her surprise after years of infertility and being told that she likely wouldn't ever have her own child! It had taken her years to come to terms with the fact that she would likely be childless, but she'd made the most of it by taking her life in a different direction. After finding out she probably wouldn't be able to have children, she decided to go all in on her dream job as a platform artist, traveling somewhere new and exciting every week to share her knowledge with the rest of the beauty industry that she loves. She had only been in Houston for a month when she found out she was pregnant. At the time, she had private insurance that cost about $1,000 a month but no secondary insurance. She had just started over in a new salon in a new city and managed to keep traveling across the country almost every weekend until a month prior to delivery. Imagine flying and renting cars every week while pregnant and carrying two heavy suitcases, a backpack, and a tripod! She knew she needed to work as much as possible before the birth of her daughter because she wanted to take six months off from traveling, especially since she still didn't know anyone in the area well enough to trust them to look after her child for extended periods.

Otherwise, she didn't have a plan. She underestimated the cost of pregnancy. There were co-pays as well as things that weren't covered by insurance, like ultrasounds, prenatal vitamins, and iron pills that cost more than $200 alone. Then there were the somewhat unexpected expenses like maternity clothes, good compression socks, baby furniture, lost income due to the time she had to take out of her day for doctor's appointments, and the months of work she would miss after the birth. All of that didn't even include the expenses of housing a newborn in a city where you have no one to lean on for childcare. After her daughter was born, it didn't make sense for her to continue to work in her salon in Houston because she would've paid more for childcare than she was making behind the chair. After she was cleared to fly again, she took clients at her Missouri location once a month because she could earn more money in one week there than she would starting over in a new place while paying for childcare in Houston for the rest of the month.

If she'd had procedures lined up beforehand, she could have enjoyed her pregnancy and time off with her baby a lot more. Instead, she was so stressed about money. The expenses nearly forced her to file for bankruptcy and certainly changed the trajectory of her career. She realized then that she needed income that didn't require her physical presence or the trade-off of time for money. So, she started dabbling in network marketing. She found a lipstick she could wear and still kiss her baby without smearing it everywhere. While she loved the product, she wasn't equipped with the right leaders or training to start earning enough to make a difference just yet. Talk about stress! But then again, she still feels that God's plan is always best. If it hadn't been for experiences like this one, she wouldn't feel inspired to share her mistakes and the things she has learned along the way with others in the hopes that they won't have to learn the hard way, too.

Kylie was about to open her new salon when God blessed her with a daughter. Having a new baby and opening a brand-new salon company at the same time wasn't initially in her plans, but hey—sometimes that's how the cookie crumbles, and sometimes those shifts in life turn out to be the biggest blessings. Kylie's second child—her son—came almost twenty-four days early. Happy April Fools' Day! The joke was on her, and with her having a type A personality, this didn't sit well with her and her plans.

We are sharing all of this with you because so many women like ourselves get caught off guard like this. We cannot stress enough how important it is to have an amazing support system during these times. If you don't have other income sources or a great health insurance plan, pregnancy can leave you in a real pickle. Adding on to your family is expensive. In addition to health insurance copays, you've got to buy different medicines and supplements, ultrasounds, new bras every month, new clothes, nursery furniture, and everything a baby needs. There are so many things to do to prepare for a baby, and don't get us started on childcare costs and the havoc it might wreak on your work schedule when you think you're ready to get back out there.

Switching gears a bit, let's talk about illness and other major, unseen curveballs. In 2023, Kylie was diagnosed with triple-negative breast cancer. No one is ever prepared for a diagnosis of cancer, but there it was. Before you worry too much, let us reassure you that she absolutely kicked its ass! She aligned herself with a higher power and knew that she had much more to do and share. She knew she wasn't kept here to be mediocre but to be extraordinary. In fact, many of her thoughts in this book were conceptualized during her time spent in chemotherapy sessions, in which she had long stretches of stillness and quiet reflection. She has had an incredible amount of mindset training and knows that what we focus on grows. So, instead of focusing on the negative, she affirmed daily to herself that all of this would have zero power over her, then chose to release it and focus on the positive.

> *"I can do all things through Christ, who strengthens me."*
> *– (Philippians 4:13)*

Her nurses and her oncologist at Texas Oncology would agree that her mindset was a game changer. She believes down to her core that this is why she had very little to no side effects and was able to carry on a fairly normal life during that year. She served her amazing clients, ran a salon company, attended all her children's activities, coached cheerleading for her daughter, rode dirt bikes with her son and horses with her Sunday crew, and didn't miss a football or a baseball game. She was extremely grateful this happened to her, and not one of her children or another loved one. Why? Because she knew she could take it.

And even when she had to cut one day from her workweek, she managed to make more than she did the year before. Perhaps focusing on the right thoughts and the right services—think high-ticket items such as extensions—

helped. Giving gratitude became a weekly practice. Imagine if all you had today was what you gave gratitude for yesterday; then think about what we covered in Chapter 1. The reality is that a lot of people aren't that lucky, and a lot of people have awful experiences with cancer. A lot of people would have had to take off work for an entire year, which would have left them financially devastated. If you think daily expenses are tough, consider what it would feel like to stare down the barrel at CT scans, MRIs, ultrasounds, biopsies, sixteen rounds of chemo, four major surgeries, and countless doctor's appointments with co-pays. The list goes on and on.

Fortunately, Kylie's husband has wonderful medical benefits with his employer, but that isn't the case for everyone. This is why we would highly suggest that you invest in a major medical policy and possibly even a secondary insurance policy. There are even some policies out there that would cover at least part of your income while you're unable to work due to these kinds of circumstances. Go to an insurance professional so they can give you the ins and outs of all the plans and coverages, as well as their costs. If you think you can't afford any of that, consider that you can probably get a decent plan for about $500 a month. That breaks down to about $125 a week. If you work five days a week, that's about $25 a day. So, maybe you want to decide you want to use your tip money to pay for your health insurance.

Maybe you want to double down and go for life insurance and mutual funds or an indexed universal life (IUL) insurance policy. If you paid $1,000 per month for both combined, that's $50 a day for every day that you work. An indexed universal life insurance policy offers a cash value component along with a death benefit. Unlike a 401(k) or an IRA, you aren't penalized for taking out money early or if you choose to use the money for something else, such as retirement. Lots of people use these policies for their children, too.

No one thinks about this while they're young and healthy, but it's never a bad time to prepare and protect yourself and your family. People don't plan to fail; they fail to plan.

Now, let's chat about home ownership. If that's something you desire, what do you visualize as your home, your sanctuary? This is different for everyone, but no matter what it looks like to you, it's safe to say that there needs to be a plan in place to make your vision a reality. If you're planning to purchase a home, you should aim to have roughly 20% of the total asking price as a down payment. Play around with some potential prices to determine what you can feasibly save for this expense.

Here's the catch: when you want to buy a home, you have to be able to show your income, and unless you're a W-2 employee, you are responsible for claiming your taxes each year. We really think Google's numbers are quite low in terms of what the average hairstylist makes these days: a whopping $28,000 to $36,000 a year! To be fair, our profession is notorious for burying cash. We personally think that's because a lot of people aren't reporting all of what they make behind the chair, which is crazy because when you go to buy a pricey item like a house or a car, it looks like you don't make much money. We know better because we are Six-Figure Stylists living extraordinary lives. We are a marvelously talented group of people that many in the general population think are a bunch of uneducated losers who couldn't hack it in college. But numbers don't lie, so we highly recommend reporting all of your income and seeking out a tax professional as needed, but also putting away at least 20% in anticipation of tax season. There are even tax courses you can take to learn more. Tax company Hey Taxi offers membership and training for female entrepreneurs which really helped Lacey learn to be smarter about this topic.

The average salon owner makes between $92,000 and $145,000 a year, so if you want to propel yourself to the next level, you may consider becoming a salon owner. But, as you will have noted in the earlier chapters of this book, it's not that easy, and it's a lot of responsibility. Truthfully, most new businesses close within the first year of being open. This is usually because there wasn't a clear and concise plan or budgeting guidelines in place beforehand. What you've read of our experiences in this arena so far should have impressed upon you, as we both have made some really big mistakes that we hope you can avoid. However, we've also done our fair share of avoiding mistakes and pain points because we sought out someone who had already done what we hoped to accomplish and asked for guidance. There's absolutely no need to reinvent the wheel; someone else has been there, done it, and is willing to mentor you. So, educate yourself, get a plan together, hire a coach or find a mentor, and talk to other professionals in this area before you make life-changing decisions.

All of the above is part of what it means to be financially smart. In our business, it also means figuring out what you love to do and then specializing in it. Being the expert in a particular service versus a generalist makes you stand out. You don't want to be the jack-of-all-trades and the master of none. If you are truly passionate about something, that energy will translate to your work, and you will be successful.

When it comes to budgeting in your salon, whether you're the owner or a suite owner, there are lots of things you can do to remain profitable. We highly recommend having a separate bank account(s), maybe even with a separate bank (out of sight, out of mind), into which you could move that 20% for taxes. Pay yourself a commission (50% if you're unsure to start with) using an actual check that you can turn around and put in your personal account. Leave the remainder of the money (about 30%) in your business account. Use your business account to pay for things like rent, supplies, marketing, classes, and anything you need for your business.

Total Earnings = 20% (taxes) + 50% (commission) + 30% (business expenses)

That's going to make it so much easier when you do your taxes; you won't have to rifle through a box of receipts from five different bank accounts and all your credit cards. Download an app to track your mileage to any business-related location because that adds up just like any other deductible expense. In our experience, hiring a bookkeeper to come in once a month and keep everything organized is worth its weight in gold! Whether you're an independent stylist or a salon owner, it's vital to know if you're profitable or not. So, keep business and personal accounts separate and budget for independence. You have to know what percentage of your money is going where.

If you're selling retail products, what percent of the budget replenishes that stock? We don't recommend just buying anything you want. There needs to be a purpose and a plan. Remember that most salons aren't thriving unless they're retailing; salons that aren't retailing are dying slowly. That being said, don't expect to sell too much if you only have one of each product on the shelf. As a general rule, if you want to sell six of one product, you must have twelve on the shelf. One or two of each product just isn't enough to put the consumer in a shopping mindset. They go to places like Ulta or Sephora because those retailers always have loads of inventory. They also send coupons, regularly host promotions, give rewards to their customers just for buying something there, use eye-catching endcap displays, and have small impulse items near the registers.

These stores visually prepare a person to get into shopping mode; they have baskets or bags at the door for shoppers to load up with purchases. They invite the shopper to try out certain items before they buy them. The shelves should look neat and aesthetically pleasing. They also sometimes promote products in different areas of the store: think hot tools with heat stylers and other things that ought to be featured next to each other. There's a reason these stores are known for selling beauty products, while most salons struggle to sell the same things. The products need to be managed often, not left to collect dust. No one is attracted to dusty items that look stale on the shelf or a messy area. We like the two-finger rule when it comes to placement. Simply put, there should be enough space for two fingers to fit between the top of a product and the underside of the shelf above it. This gives your shoppers a logical layout to peruse while maximizing your shelf space. We also like to have the same rule of separation between products. We encourage you to think about how you could enhance your clients' shopping experience to be a more inviting one.

In Lacey's experience, having regular promotions with a lot of products on the shelf is absolutely vital. There's nothing like seeing loads of shiny new products on a big display in the middle of the room that every guest has to walk around to boost retail sales! Your retail-to-service sales (RTS) percentage depends on this. We also cross-promote so people continue to see those products throughout the salon and spa.

Lacey actually stopped shopping at one particular store that we won't name. While she has nothing against this store—and particularly liked that they have mommy and me clothing—every time she went in, the store was just a mess. The displays were always dug through, and the clothing was left unfolded and disheveled. It was unattractive and made it hard to find things that she liked. Quite frankly, it was overstimulating for someone with ADD. The anxious, uneasy feeling she gets when she is in a messy environment always makes her want to leave. It certainly didn't invite her to stay longer and shop.

While we are talking about money, we'd like to propose that too many beauty professionals are leaving money on the table. There are several tax credits available now, especially after the pandemic, although many of them have always been there—we just weren't as aware of them. For example, if you were an independent in 2020 and 2021 and had COVID-19, there is the self-employment tax credit. So many of us had to take time off because we were exposed to COVID-19 at work; under the Families First Coronavirus Response Act (FFCRA), there are self-employment tax credits available to you. It's hard to get loans right now, as interest rates are currently high. And even if they aren't, by the time you read this, there could be money sitting there, waiting for you to pick it up, but it's already been allocated elsewhere. If there was a briefcase of cash with your name on it sitting in a parking lot, you'd go get it, wouldn't you? There are research and development grants for business owners that have been around for decades. These could perhaps be used to expand your business, or try something new. Either way, this is money you don't have to pay back. You never know if you don't look into it. We will have a resource at the end of this chapter if you'd like to learn more about different tax credits that you may qualify for.

Smart financing includes insurance savings plans for salon owners. If you own a business with W-2 employees, there are ways that you can save as much as $500 a year per employee. This way, your employees can have better benefits or even add-on insurance and more money on their paychecks. We are the only trade whose students pay to go to school and aren't guaranteed a decent hourly wage and health insurance, life insurance, or retirement plans. Most trades are unionized; there is a union for us, but to our knowledge, it's mostly only active in California to service professionals working for movie sets and the like, not for commission-based or hourly employees. We suspect this is because when most trades were unionized, cosmetology could've been left out due to it being primarily a female industry. Most hairstylists and beauty professionals have to do all of this on their own or simply go without. Sadly, most of us are not taught this in cosmetology schools.

So many things fall under the category of smart financial planning. There isn't a lot of difference between working in a commission-based salon and how you get paid as a hairstylist compared to working for yourself and renting a booth. So, let us break it down for you. When you're working as an employee in a commission-based salon, the average commission is between 45% and 55%. Most of the time, the salon owner is doing all of the marketing. They're paying the bills. They're taking out the taxes for you. They provide your educational opportunities. If you're at a good place, they're also providing you with vacation pay. You can still take advantage of tax breaks if you own a home-based business (such as those affiliate marketing opportunities we discussed earlier). If you rent a booth, you're still probably going to pay yourself about 50%, but you're also responsible for all of the overhead, purchasing, and booking. You're responsible for the marketing, which is great if you are a disciplined person and can do that as well as budget. The tax benefits of owning your own business are nice if you know what you're doing. We've personally experienced all of this as salon and spa owners, commission-based stylists, and booth rental stylists. So, we'll do our best to break it down for you.

After Lacey sold her salon and spa, she went to work at a commission-based salon for two years. The salon provided a lot of good education that she would have had to pay for otherwise. She thought not having all of the owner's responsibilities would be like a breath of fresh air—and it was. She was given a lot of empty promises, though. She was told that she would have a flexible schedule, would not be required to perform certain services, and would have an associate since she was used to working with one and had so many clients at the time that she needed one in order to continue booking the same way. All of this really affected her business. She became an educator during this time, and it was impossible to make up for the missed time, especially without the extra set of hands she was used to having. She actually came back from a trip to learn that her associate had been put on the floor because they had lost more trained stylists. This cheated the associate out of the training she would have received and robbed Lacey of a replacement, which is a total nightmare for a busy stylist who was used to never running late.

If you own a salon, you have to keep the promises you make. Regardless of your role, get it in writing. If you're an owner, it doesn't benefit you to force people to do services they don't like. They won't do a good job or want to stay working for you. Something Lacey learned is that it pays to be flexible with people's schedules. People will work harder when they want to be there and when they know they can get the time off they need. This may require hiring more people or shifting schedules, but this is an industry where most people need the freedom of flexibility—especially because much of our time behind the chair takes place during the evenings and on weekends. Something else we've learned is that while events are fantastic, you can overdo it when it comes to how much you're expecting of your staff. It won't always work for everyone's schedule, and no event is more important than missing their kid's programs at school, for instance. The people who want to work and make money will. It's that simple, and it can't be forced.

After leaving this salon, Lacey rented a station at another salon, and for the most part, it was absolutely incredible. All she had to do was get a renter's license. The salon had a really smart layout and took care of the retail. All of the stylists could make a commission on products sold. Having so much retail in their store also meant that there were a lot of opportunities for education. Unfortunately, renters never seem to want to take time off their books to get educated. However, this rental business allowed Lacey to claim a lot of write-offs and tax deductions that she couldn't at her commission-based salon. These salon owners seemed to genuinely care for their people; most people rented a chair, but everyone was their own boss. The owners were there for support and anything they needed. They also had a "stylist closet" from which renters could purchase products with their weekly rent. Due to the size of the account, the distributor was able to give them a discount on back-bar goods. They upcharged it to the stylists, and the salon carried the overhead. They had everything in stock that the staff could possibly need, including color, developers, gloves, foil, and treatments. The flexibility and freedom that this salon offered kept people happy and wanting to stay. That being said, many of the stylists peaked there. It's hard to be self-motivated, and some people need a push to do more. If that's you, we recommend getting a mentor or a coach. Accountability is key. In our experience, it's also best to have a tribe of people to motivate you and to inspire you to keep growing. There is danger in the comfort zone.

After moving to Texas, Lacey worked in a commission-based salon. It was in a fantastic location, with incredible structure and organization, as well as flexibility. She started in a new town and had pretty full books within her first couple of weeks, which isn't always the case! This salon was set up well; the retail was on point, and everyone's numbers reflected it. They had three locations, were branded well, and were active in their communities. They had incredible educational opportunities, including coaching and mentoring.

This salon company helped many stylists fulfill their dreams of becoming traveling educators and provided editorial and fashion week opportunities. They also had a shareholder program so stylists could own part of a successful salon company without all of the guesswork. The owner could take a step back and give the shareholders more responsibility and pay in addition to an exit strategy. This also helped to retain those stylists who would otherwise want to eventually own a salon or suite of their own.

    Your rent on a suite is likely going to be higher, but you can offset that with retail sales. And, if you are a killer at sales and smart about budgeting and how you order your products, plus you take advantage of every possible tax deduction, you will likely be able to make more money in the long run. You can be smart about your money, but if you're currently in a commission-based situation and think that the salon owner is making so much off of your services, you're dead wrong. Salon owners assume all the risk and responsibility, and they have to have professional liability insurance. When you rent a suite, there are also more licenses to obtain: a salon owner license from the state board, sales tax permits if you sell retail, and city licenses to be able to operate in your town. You also are responsible for cleaning and doing all your own laundry, including all your towels and capes. You're responsible for booking all of your own appointments, and if you're not careful in a suite rental situation, it's easy to forget that you are the only one running your business. If you're used to having someone else run the business for you from an employee standpoint or even in a booth situation, this is going to be an eye-opener for you. It's no longer just you coming in and slaying amazing hair all day.

    Lacey rented a salon suite after her twelve-year lease was terminated, and she'd live-streamed an event on Facebook where she was asked to speak about her collagen experience. It was an honor to be asked, but unfortunately, the salon company she worked for at the time was not happy about her statement regarding how she felt that collagen was the most revolutionary beauty product on the market. After the initial shock and hurt, she decided that God had closed a door that she wouldn't have closed on her own. And what an upgrade! The suite was absolutely gorgeous. After renting for twelve years at the same location, she figured she would just move her stuff over, but she also got to decorate the suite, which was both exciting and expensive. She discovered she needed different city licenses and had to file with the state board for salon owner licensing. Different inspections needed to take place. She hired a certified public accountant (CPA) to help her file for an LLC and an EIN. She learned that one should run their business through an entity with an EIN instead of a social security number like she'd done as a sole proprietor because, on the off chance that someone tried to sue her, they would only be able to sue the business, not her. She had to get a license to purchase retail items to sell, as well as set up payments to pay the sales tax with the Internal Revenue Service (IRS). She purchased things like salon towels, capes, gloves, laundry detergent, hand soap, cleaning products, a mini fridge, shelves, a trash can and bags, drinks, snacks, new business cards, storage for color and other products, shampoo and conditioner, waxing supplies, and furniture. Then she got around to purchasing retail.

Opening a suite is like opening a mini salon. She was quite surprised by how much it added up to, and how much one can fit into a tiny suite. These are all things that one doesn't have to consider when renting a chair or working in a commission-based salon. If you're planning to open a suite, we recommend saving up for these things ahead of time instead of purchasing them little by little along the way. It's hard to buy ahead until you know what the suite looks like and what you can do with the space.

Be honest with yourself about what kind of person you are. Are you disciplined? Are you better off letting someone else assume risks and responsibilities? Has it always been your dream to own your own business, and are you willing to take the challenge? Are you willing to work when you don't have clients? The average stylist now seems to work about three days a week, and we think that's great. It means we can have flexibility within our personal and professional schedules. Just know that if the only time you come in is when you have clients, then you're not making time for new ones. In our experience, that type of stylist doesn't put in the extra time for education, and they're not willing to stay late. However, if you are required to be somewhere working for somebody else, you have more opportunities for earning and retailing. Ask yourself, *Am I just working or am I also working on my business?* If you're not as busy as you want to be, consider that when we come into the salon and take guests, that's working *in* your business. Working *on* your business creates more business, which in turn helps *retain* business.

Think of things you can do to enhance your business or bring more in. This sometimes means tracking, planning, and categorizing your client list. You could give your place a makeover or rearrange the retail. If you clean your own salon, go outside and come back in with "client's eyes" (what a client would see) to see what you might have missed. When we work there and see it every day, we sometimes overlook the dust hanging off vents and ceiling fans or that paint needs to be touched up. Another way you can work on your business is by promoting yourself online or in person. Get involved in your local chamber of commerce or other business networking groups to stay in front of your local community. Stylists can get so busy that they forget to promote themselves or think they no longer need to. This is a common mistake, and if you're not careful, things will start falling apart.

A couple of salon retail secrets we want to let you in on are SalonScale and Vish. If any of you are using these pieces of software, then you know that they will help you offset your back-bar costs and tell you exactly how much each service costs to perform on your clients. They essentially turn your back-bar into a profit center of its own, allowing you to charge the client for the products used on their hair, down to the penny. Think of it as parts and labor. The client pays for the "part," and you perform the "labor." Professional goods cost more nowadays, and the beauty industry is no exception. Kylie used SalonScale, and in one year, she was able to add $117,000 to her bottom line. If you work in a salon and your owner is begging stylists to sell retail, it's because they want to remain profitable in order to keep the doors open for their employees and their guests.

Salons typically only make 3% off services but get 50% off retail items. If they're paying stylists a commission on these, then they may only profit about 30%. So, if you think that salon owners are making all their money from services, they're not. Salons that don't sell retail aren't staying open.

We highly recommend the profit-first method, which teaches you to pay yourself first and put the rest of the money aside where you can't reach it so easily. The Bible also teaches us to give the first 10% of what we make to God, then save 10% (Matthew 25:14-30). We highly suggest getting financially educated so you can learn how you can invest your money in things that will be there for you in the future. Unfortunately, bills never stop coming in, but the money stops coming in when we stop working or if we aren't prepared.

> *"A good man leaves an inheritance to his children's children, but the sinner's wealth is laid up for the righteous."*
> *– (Proverbs 13:22)*

The wealthy have been using specific policies for years to create generational wealth. At the end of this chapter, we will have a resource for you to learn more or book a consultation to see if this is a good fit for you. Being financially prepared for when life throws us curveballs is so smart. It's no coincidence that the average millionaire has at least seven or eight income streams.

> *"Divide your portion to seven, or even eight, for you do not know what misfortune may occur on the earth."*
> *– (Ecclesiastes 11:12)*

Now, let's talk about exit strategies. We all need to have a plan for retirement. As a traveling educator, Lacey has met so many beauty professionals who desperately want to retire but cannot. Sometime back, she met a ninety-five-year-old lady behind the chair. She loved her craft and her salon guests, and her salon family was wonderful enough to look out for her. We don't know her whole story, and we suppose her career keeps her active, but Lacey also noticed her shoulders and back were slumped and couldn't help but wonder if she hadn't retired because she simply couldn't.

We also have friends in their sixties and seventies who are still behind the chair. One in particular recently reached out for help. Her body is tired; she is scared and doesn't know what to do because she wasn't taught to plan for the future, and now she is struggling financially. She is at an age where, unfortunately, a lot of younger people don't want to go to her, and a lot of her former salon guests are now gone. She is faced with an unknown future and has to either get a second job or learn a new skill that she can physically handle and that pays her enough. This stylist is very talented and willing to work but doesn't have the clientele or the classes that used to pay her regularly. Unfortunately, at least in the beauty industry, it seems like when a female gets older, there is always a younger one with less experience who can be paid less than a seasoned artist. This is one of the biggest reasons we felt called to write this book.

For example, Tina is a fifty-one-year-old mother of four and a very talented stylist who used to work in Lacey's salon. She has been in this industry for thirty years. Her business is declining (which I've experienced is normal after turning forty-five), she is divorced, and is the only person in her home who can contribute financially. She is depressed and feels hopeless about her future. She has more than one job and thought that at this point in her life, she would be able to slow down. She will likely have to move out of the home where she raised her children, and she is just trying to stay afloat. She never thought about retirement and wasn't taught how to plan for the future in a financial sense. Each time she had one of her children, she said that it set her back.

Retirement for beauty professionals isn't unfathomable, but if you're banking on help with this from a salon owner, we recommend taking charge of your finances now. Let's face it: Social Security just isn't going to be around much longer, and you need to invest in something that you can use as a retirement plan. The earlier you start, the better. Money saved that you never really see is the best kind of saving; if it's in our savings accounts, we can access it too easily. A lot of financial experts refer to cash in your savings account as "dead money." The stock market is a gamble you probably don't want to take on your future. We are not saying don't invest in the stock market; just don't bet your whole future on it. You may consider investing in things like gold or silver, real estate properties, or other passive, more stable income sources. Think of things that will continuously pay you. Robert T. Kiyosaki says to look at everything you buy as an asset or a liability. If you pay for it, it's a liability. If someone else pays for it, it's an asset.

"It's not how much money you make, but how much money you keep, how hard it works for you, and how many generations you keep it for."
–Robert T. Kiyosaki

A salon owner may have the luxury of selling the business in shares or as the physical location, although most salons we come across have no clue how to go about that. As a hairstylist, you can't sell the clients even if you have your own business. So, you have to prepare for the future in other ways. There are so many people across this country who don't have the financial means to retire. It's really smart to start on this at the very beginning of your career and get yourself on a plan as well as know how to protect your assets.

"The richest people in the world look for and build networks; everyone else looks for work."
– Robert T. Kiyosaki

A salon owner will have a lot more options than an independent hairstylist or beauty professional. If you're a salon owner, you can sell your salon if you've run your business in such a way that it's still profitable and worth something. Make sure your tax returns reflect a successful company. If you're not profiting on paper, nobody wants to buy your business. Someone looking to purchase your salon company will typically need a couple of years of tax returns to reference, profit and loss analyses, and balance sheets. If your salon isn't profitable, then you have nothing to sell besides assets; Kylie purchased her second salon location this way and assumed the lease of the previous owner. Another option is to sell your salon in small chunks through shareholders. This is a great exit strategy for profitable salons because the shareholders gain partial ownership of the salon. People care more about the things they own and are invested in than if they're just coming to work for someone else. Think about when you were a kid, and maybe your parents would say things like, "You know, I paid for that." When others pay for little pieces of your salon, of your dream, they buy into their own dream and care about it. This will have a trickle-down effect on the rest of the staff, who will take ownership in their own ways.

Have you considered using a stockbroker or a financial advisor to help you manage money that you have put away to grow? This could be in an IUL, stocks, IRAs, 401(k)s, high-yield savings accounts and bonds, or a certificate of deposit (CD) account. You have to let the money go to work for you, so do some research and educate yourself. Get creative; no one said you have to grow your financial portfolio traditionally. Who knows? Maybe you'll find something that you think would be a smart business or passive stream of income, even if you aren't ready to retire. The opportunities are endless if your mind is open to them. Or, if you've built up your affiliate marketing streams, you could have residual passive income coming in. You just have to be intentional, strategic, and smart. Nothing happens by accident.

When Lacey got married at the age of nineteen, her husband had a 401(k), and they thought it would be enough for them both to retire on, but let's just be real here for a minute. Even if most marriages don't end in divorce (and that one did), a 401(k) alone is not enough for one person to retire on, let alone two. Don't count on a spouse for your retirement. Lacey started investing in mutual funds attached to a whole life insurance policy. Having a mom who was terminally ill and who eventually passed at the age of fifty-seven led her to attach a long-term care rider to that policy and to better appreciate why this type of policy is important. Nursing homes and in-home health care don't come free. Lacey and her siblings provided this physical and financial care for her mother when Lacey was in her twenties and due to her mom's illness, her policy paid the premiums that her mom wouldn't otherwise be able to afford.

Later, Lacey invested in a Roth IRA with some of the money that she received from her mom's life insurance policy. While this will compound, to this day, one can only invest $6,000 a year into this type of account, or $7,000 if you're older than fifty. Mutual funds and IRAs are typically safe investments, but when the market has gains, you make money, and when the market tanks, so can your retirement fund. As a younger stylist, Lacey thought this and Social Security would be enough. Now, she isn't so sure that the latter will be around much longer, nor does she believe one should depend on the government or their employer for financial security. She recently invested in an IUL policy, and while some people think about life insurance as money to leave for their loved ones after they are gone (which we think is good, too), this type of policy can also be used to retire on without compromising one's death benefits.

In addition to her affiliate marketing income, Lacey owns other passive income sources. She uses these to invest in other things to keep her money working for her and is always open to expanding her portfolio. She has strategic plans for the money she makes and enjoys investing in the stock market, though she does not think the stock market is the basket in which she should put all of her eggs. It's a gamble, and you should never gamble what you can't afford to lose.

Six-Figure Stylist Takeaways: (Scan the QR code at the end of the chapter to access "Bonus Resources")

- What can you do today to secure your retirement?
- What can you do today to prepare for your future health needs?
- What tax benefits can you take advantage of that you haven't in the past?
- Increase profits in your salon through retail revenue.

This salon owner checklist (which can be used for suites as well) is a baseline and may be different according to your local requirements, so check your city and state policies before applying it to your business practices.

- LLC and an EIN
- City business license
- License to retail
- Salon license
- Professional insurance

"Bonus Resources" to enhance your experience.

- Life Insurance and retirement planning consultation
- Health Insurance

PLEASE SCAN THE QR CODE TO ACCESS:

Resources:

- *Profit First: Transform Your Business from a Cash-Eating Monster to a Money-Making Machine* by Mike Michalowicz
- The Bible

CHAPTER 9
TAKE MEANINGFUL ACTION

Six-Figure Stylists think big and believe in themselves. Your income is a direct reflection of your mindset.

"Extremity expands your capacity."
– Ed Mylett

You will never surpass where you think you can go. Once you have a big thought, take action. Be honest with yourself about how much effort you're putting into your endeavors. In this book, we've discussed the grit and sacrifice required for success. What price are you willing to pay? Take a look at your daily habits. Where and how are you spending your time? Actions don't lie.

When we work harder in the gym, our bodies get stronger, they get leaner, and they build up our endurance. When we spend time working on our business, it gets stronger and more successful. When we spend time working on our marriage or relationships, they get better.

"Action speaks louder than words but not nearly as often."
– Mark Twain

Take daily actions to help you reach your goals because success is found in our daily habits. If you're binge-watching Netflix every day, we encourage you to ask yourself what value that's adding to your life. Are the things you're doing every day, even when no one's watching, bringing you closer to where you want to go or farther away?

Don't just write down your goals and think about them. Take action as soon as you have the idea so you don't lose momentum. We believe that the good Lord put it in your head and in your heart for a reason. Do you ever think of texting or calling a person and letting them know you're thinking about them? Trust that the Divine has put that thought there for a reason and make the call or send the text. You never know what that could do for a person; you could save a friend's life without even knowing it. When you hear that voice that tells you that you can't do something, or to be realistic, that voice is the enemy. Realism almost never equals greatness. Decide who you are going to listen to and act accordingly.

We invite you to pause and write down what's holding you back. Start with one thing you need to let go of; when you release it, you can replace it with something better. The sweet taste of success all starts with a thought. Either you think you can, or you think you can't, but either way, you are right. You are the perfectly capable writer of your own story. If the people around you think your dream is too big, form a new circle. Don't let negativity bog you down. Just because no one else has done something before doesn't mean it can't be done. When Alexander Graham Bell invented the first telephone in 1876, a lot of people probably didn't believe it was possible to speak to someone from so far away. Now, we can't imagine life without our phones. We can be anywhere in the world and FaceTime anyone else who has a phone. We can look up anything we want to without opening a single book or flipping through an encyclopedia. You never know what the trickle-down effect of your thoughts and actions will be.

It wasn't that many years ago that salon suites were first introduced, but then mini salons started popping up everywhere and changed our industry.

How can you leave the world a better place, or revolutionize our industry for the better? Maybe your idea is not even industry-related, and that's fine. We all have hopes and dreams of our own; it's what we do with them that matters. Those who are bold enough to go for them end up with the most profit, even if sometimes the profit comes later. Sometimes we fail; that's part of the process. When you get bucked off a horse, you get back on, or you'll never be a great rider. Celebrate your failures as steps closer to success. By virtue of the process of elimination, now you know what doesn't work. It took Thomas Edison countless failed attempts to create the light bulb, but he also learned all the ways that the concept of them didn't work.

Lacey keeps a notebook by her bed for when she wakes up in the middle of the night and has a brilliant idea. If we don't write those kinds of ideas down, we almost never remember them. But there are more times now that Lacey will get up and take action after she's jotted something down. Don't let that inspiration go to waste.

When we decided to team up and start Beauty Concierge, we held brainstorming sessions, mapped out what we wanted it to look like and the difference we wanted to make, and booked a call with our branding specialist to discuss it all. We researched related topics, scheduled meetings to iron it all out, and created our LLC right away. We started manifesting and visualizing what our success would look like, and really felt what it would be like to change the lives of so many people in this industry that we love so much. We were on the phone one day discussing our ideas and thought process, and Kylie said, "Let's call Cris (our publisher) right now."

We took immediate action and met with the publishing company right away for this book. We didn't wait, and each time we finished a call, we'd plan the next one as well as our next steps. We often met early in the morning just to suit everyone's schedules. The most successful people we know get up that early anyway. We immediately sowed seeds because we know that we reap what we sow. Lacey booked a flight to meet Kylie because we had actually never met in person prior to this, and there was no time like the present to record the manuscript for this book. We planned our time together beforehand in order to maximize it. We planned our content and parts of our courses while we were together. We hit the ground running each day with intentional schedules and built-in downtime so we could recharge our batteries.

The bigger the risk, the greater the reward, and without some risk, there is no reward. Are you currently settling? Are you going to look back at your life and say you gave it your all, or will you wonder why you didn't go for your dreams? Maybe you aren't giving your all to your marriage, your kids, or your career, but you know what you could do to make it better. Don't wait until tomorrow to get started; we are never promised tomorrow. All we have is right now, so you have to decide you no longer want to tolerate what you currently have. Be grateful, but dream bigger.

Six-Figure Stylist Takeaways:

- Think big and visualize your idea.
- Take immediate action. Don't let your idea get stale.
- Take a look at your life and determine what must go, what stays, and what you can do to reach your goals that much sooner.
- Do you have a calling that you have been holding back on?
- Never forget that diamonds are made from withstanding pressure. Are you ready to shine?

Resources:

- *The Power of One More* by Ed Mylett
- *The 10X Rule* by Grant Cardone

FINAL THOUGHTS...

We thank you from the bottom of our hearts for taking time out of your busy life to read this book. Our hope is that you not only found value in these pages but learned from our discoveries. We want to empower you with the tools to take charge of your life and your business. We invite you to embark on this exciting journey with Beauty Concierge, dive into our courses, and sign up for a membership that includes monthly content, ongoing educational opportunities, personal growth resources, and one-on-one customized coaching that comes complete with an affiliate program to help you share this valuable information with your friends and earn your investment back. You are destined for greatness, and we're here to help guide you every step of the way.

Find us on Instagram at:
@officialbeautyconcierge
@laceybroocke
@kylielynnep
@kyliephillippihair

Join us on Facebook:
Beauty Concierge
Kylie Lynne Phillippi
Lacey Broocke

THANK YOU FOR READING OUR BOOK!

WE HAVE PRESENTED MANY BONUS RESOURCES AT THE END OF CHAPTERS. THIS IS A REMINDER TO:

SCAN THE QR CODE TO ACCESS THEM ALL.

We appreciate your interest in our book, and value your feedback as it helps us improve future versions of this book. We would appreciate it if you could leave your invaluable review on Amazon.com with your feedback. Thank you!

www.ingramcontent.com/pod-product-compliance
Lightning Source LLC
LaVergne TN
LVHW051838080426
835512LV00018B/2940